REFLECTING ON REALITY

Tavistock Clinic Series

Margot Waddell (Series Editor)

Published and distributed by Karnac Books

Orders

Tel: +44 (0)20 8969 4454; Fax: +44 (0)20 8969 5585
Email: shop@karnacbooks.com
www.karnacbooks.com

REFLECTING ON REALITY

Psychotherapists at Work in Primary Care

Edited by

John Launer, Sue Blake, & Dilys Daws

KARNAC

LONDON   NEW YORK

First published in 2005 by
H. Karnac (Books) Ltd.
6 Pembroke Buildings, London NW10 6RE

British Library Cataloguing in Publication Data

A C.I.P. for this book is available from the British Library

ISBN: 1-85575-211-5

10 9 8 7 6 5 4 3 2 1

Edited, designed, and produced by Communication Crafts

Printed in the United Kingdom by Hobbs the Printers Ltd, Totton, Hampshire

www.karnacbooks.com

CONTENTS

ACKNOWLEDGEMENTS

The editors wish to thank Lucy Ettinger on the GP Unit at the Tavistock Clinic for her secretarial and administrative help which has been, as always, unfailingly conscientious and efficient. They would also like to express their gratitude to the staff of the Clinic library for much assistance during the preparation of this book. Authors of individual chapters would like to thank the following:

Dilys Daws (chapter 2) thanks the James Wigg Practice for giving her standing room.

Beverley Tydeman and Patrick Kiernan (chapter 3) acknowledge with thanks the contribution of Dayle Thackray who was instrumental in initiating the project and whose thinking has influenced their chapter. They would also like to thank Dr Adrian Raby, who took responsibility for the audit data.

Rob Senior and Robert Mayer (chapter 4) would like to acknowledge the ongoing contributions of the Highgate Family Clinic team members Hilary Graham, Irene Bard, Myrna Lazarus, and Penny Louden.

Sara Barratt (chapter 5) thanks Dr Jack Czauderna and his patients for giving permission to describe their work together and for giving her the opportunity to learn from them about collaboration in general practice.

Jenny Altschuler (chapter 6) wishes to thank the primary care team of the practice described in her chapter for supporting this work and agreeing to the publication.

Cathy Urwin (chapter 8) wishes to thank particularly, among the many people who have contributed to the work described, the Sure Start team, Linda Dawson and Ferelyth Watt, other members of the Under Fives discussion group, and Dilys Daws.

SERIES EDITOR'S PREFACE

Since it was founded in 1920, the Tavistock Clinic has developed a wide range of developmental approaches to mental health which have been strongly influenced by the ideas of psychoanalysis. It has also adopted systemic family therapy as a theoretical model and a clinical approach to family problems. The Clinic is now the largest training institution in Britain for mental health, providing postgraduate and qualifying courses in social work, psychology, psychiatry, and child, adolescent, and adult psychotherapy, as well as in nursing and primary care. It trains about 1,400 students each year in over 45 courses.

The Clinic's philosophy aims at promoting therapeutic methods in mental health. Its work is based on the clinical expertise that is also the basis of its consultancy and research activities. The aim of this Series is to make available to the reading public the clinical, theoretical, and research work that is most influential at the Tavistock Clinic. The Series sets out new approaches in the understanding and treatment of psychological disturbance in children, adolescents, and adults, both as individuals and in families.

The publication of *Reflecting on Reality* is timely in several respects. In exploring and describing the interface between psychotherapeutic work and primary care, it not only makes available an area of commitment in the Tavistock of many years' standing, but it does so in the swiftly changing context of the National Health Service, as it is reconfigured and restructured in relation to the National Service Framework for Mental Health and the new Primary Care Organizations (PCOs).

The book reflects a distinctiveness and also an immense diversity of attitude and approach arising out of the thinking and experience gathered in each department of the Clinic over the years. The respective authors, each psychotherapeutically trained and each engaged, in different ways, with primary care, focus on a range of community settings in which the complex needs of patients and practitioners challenge known or standardized ways of going about things.

The emphasis is, thus, often on innovative practice and adaptation to new situations, whether in relation to working directly with general practitioners, with health visitors and practice nurses, with immigrants and refugees, or with a wide variety of services for infants, children, adolescents, and their families. In so doing, new working methodologies are evolved and vividly described with a freshness so needed in areas where painful mental states and scarce professional resources can often feel so burdensome. These pages make evident the mutual learning that can occur between psychotherapists and primary care professionals as well as health service managers, and just how much can be gained from multidisciplinary work of this kind.

Margot Waddell
August 2005

ABOUT THE EDITORS AND CONTRIBUTORS

JENNY ALTSCHULER is a consultant clinical psychologist and systemic psychotherapist, formerly based in the Child and Family Department, the Tavistock Clinic. She is currently engaged in research on migration and works as an independent psychotherapist and supervisor. In addition, she acts as consultant and trainer to a Kosova-based project, working with families affected by both political and family violence. She is the author of *Working with Families Facing Chronic Illness* (Macmillan, 1997), and her writing focuses primarily on issues related to working with families facing the transitions of illness and migration.

SARA BARRATT is a systemic psychotherapist and social worker at the Tavistock Clinic, where she is Head of Systemic Psychotherapy. She is a clinical supervisor and teacher on the Masters and Supervision courses in Systemic Psychotherapy. Sara is also member of the fostering and adoption team in the Child and Family Department, specializing in kinship care and working with families post-adoption. She has worked as a systemic psychotherapist in general practice since 1989 and has organized consultation groups and conferences on systemic practice in primary care for the Thinking Families group and for the Institute of Family Therapy.

SUE BLAKE is a GP, GP trainer, and adult psychotherapist; she is also senior clinical lecturer in general practice and Primary Care in the Adult Department of the Tavistock Clinic, having also completed training in psychiatry. Her previous research interest was in psychological responses to a diagnosis of breast cancer, and she has published several papers on this topic.

DILYS DAWS is an honorary consultant child psychotherapist at the Tavistock Clinic and visiting consultant to the baby clinic of the James Wigg Practice, Kentish Town Health Centre. She is an advisor to the Association for Infant Mental Health. Her publications include *Through the Night: Helping Parents and Sleepless Children* (Free Association Books, reprinted 1993).

NASIMA HUSSAIN is a systemic psychotherapist currently working in St Mary's Department of Child and Adolescent Psychiatry in London. She has worked for a number of years in the NHS at the Tavistock Clinic developing a therapeutic service for the Bangladeshi community, and has written a number of articles on cross-cultural work with this community. She is a tutor at the Institute of Family Therapy. Her current doctoral research is looking at changes in family life in contemporary Bangladeshi families. She is also conducting research at St Mary's on refugee families.

PATRICK KIERNAN is a GP and also a course organiser of the St Mary's GP Vocational Training Scheme, London.

JOHN LAUNER is a GP and systemic psychotherapist. He is senior clinical lecturer in general practice and primary care at the Tavistock Clinic, and Associate Director of Post Graduate GP Education at the London GP Deanery. He is the author of *Narrative Based Primary Care: A Practical Guide* (Radcliffe Medical Press, 2002) and co-editor with Jonathan Burton of *Supervision and Support in Primary Care* (Radcliffe Medical Press, 2003).

ROBERT MAYER is a GP and GP trainer in Highgate, London, and a systemic psychotherapist. He and a team of colleagues run the family clinic at the Highgate Group Practice.

Jo O'Reilly is a psychiatrist and trained in adult psychotherapy at the Tavistock Clinic. She is also training as a psychoanalyst at the Institute of Psychoanalysis.

Rob Senior is a consultant child and adolescent psychiatrist and systemic psychotherapist at the Tavistock Clinic. He is also a senior research fellow at University College London, where his research interests are in the development and evaluation of interventions to address the intergenerational transmission of psychological distress and disturbance.

Ann Simpson is a registered nurse and an adult psychotherapist. Her career in the NHS spans 40 years, and she has also worked in Switzerland and the United States. She has worked in mental health since 1977 in both the NHS and the voluntary sector and has specialized in both adult and child and family mental health. She is currently working in private practice and is a visiting tutor at the Tavistock Clinic.

Beverley Tydeman is a consultant child and adolescent psychotherapist who works at the Tavistock Clinic and the Marlborough Family Service. She has experience of working in primary care and has a particular interest in infant mental health and early intervention with families with babies or young children.

Cathy Urwin is a child and adult psychotherapist working in the NHS in East London and in private practice. She has a background in developmental psychology and has published research on early social interaction and language development in sighted and non-sighted children. She is particularly interested in work with under fives and with children with communication disorders.

REFLECTING ON REALITY

CHAPTER ONE

Introduction

John Launer

Some time ago, a GP we know was carrying out a routine morning surgery. He had a young clinical psychologist sitting in with him. She was training as a psychotherapist and wanted to learn about primary care. After the first patient of the morning had come and gone, she commented that the GP might well consider referring that person for psychotherapy. Then the second patient came and went, and the young psychotherapy trainee commented on the coincidence that the GP had now seen two successive patients who might well benefit from psychotherapy. After the next three patients, she became rather puzzled, as they also seemed to her to be eligible for psychotherapy. For the rest of the surgery she fell very quiet. The GP—an experienced practitioner—thought she had become rather depressed in the course of the morning, perhaps on account of a certain kind of cognitive dissonance. As for himself, he did not feel that she had observed a procession of candidates for psychotherapy. He felt she had simply been watching ordinary primary care and observing the human condition.

Primary care and psychotherapy are, in some very obvious ways, worlds apart. People in primary care see all comers, with a vast range of conditions and predicaments, at all times of day and night. They work at tremendous speed, seeing prodigious numbers of patients, often for only a few minutes at a time. Encounters with any individual or family can occur at unpredictable and highly variable intervals. There is often a casual and uncommitted style to consultations, which can resemble anything from a purely bureaucratic exchange to a chat between friends. The work seems uninformed by any consistent methodology for consulting, or any coherent underlying theoretical framework. The quality of emotional engagement between practitioner and patient can often be— or certainly seem—very superficial and unreflective.

By contrast, psychotherapists generally see only a very small number of patients, with a fairly narrow range of predicaments. They may see them for long, frequent, and regular sessions, perhaps over considerable periods of time. Their consulting technique is often rigorous, and it is informed by a substantial body of theoretical learning. The emotional quality of the work is usually intense, and the therapist is committed to offering focused reflection, rooted in a sustained scrutiny of both subject and self. The difference between the two worlds has been aptly summarized as "the souk and the citadel" (Wiener, 1996).

Yet in other ways primary care and psychotherapy share a great deal. The surgery and the therapist's consulting-room alike are places where people try to assign meaning to what is happening to them and seek to articulate narratives about who they are, who they might become, and who they want to be. Both are places where clinicians help people to examine the human fundamentals: birth, childhood, procreation, and death; hope and disappointment; identity and uncertainty. In both fields, practitioners strive to help patients to manage their infirmities and their mortality. In many ways, they are worlds that can learn a great deal from each other.

In this book, we present a range of work that is being done by therapists from the Tavistock Clinic who are all engaged in different ways with primary care. Our purpose is to examine what happens in the encounter between primary care and psychotherapy, both in clinical and in organizational terms. We hope to promote a discussion about the gap between primary care and psychotherapy and about the potential for creative collaboration once that gap has been bridged. Our emphasis is not on helping people in primary care to become greater enthusiasts for psychotherapy or to "make more appropriate referrals". It is on the opportunities for mutual learning that can arise when psychotherapists work alongside GPs and other primary care professionals, and on how this learning can lead to better mental health care for patients. We are interested in the interactional nature of psychotherapy attachments and in how the participants can learn about ways of thinking, ways of working, pressures and preoccupations that may be very different from their own.

Our aim in writing this book is to excite wider interest among psychotherapists, counsellors, and mental health workers generally, in developing therapeutic individual and family work in the primary care setting. We also hope to demonstrate to GPs, health visitors, practice nurses, and other members of the primary care team some of the potential that psychotherapy might offer in their workplaces, as well as encouraging health service managers to think about exploiting the their local psychotherapy services in new ways. At a time when political and structural changes in the National Health Service may be creating new opportunities to explore innovative ways of working at the interface between the two worlds (Lester, Glasby, & Tylee, 2004), we believe it is timely to offer a range of ideas from the Tavistock about how such work might be developed.

The work of the Tavistock Clinic

The Tavistock Clinic occupies a unique place in the National Health Service in Britain (Taylor, 1999). It is the largest psychotherapy outpatient clinic in the country, serving a population in and around London—and more widely for some specialized services. It offers child and adolescent mental health services (CAMHS) for a large area of north London. It is a postgraduate training institute for mental health, with a national role in training for the psychological therapies. It also provides organizational consultancy within the public sector and elsewhere, including health service institutions of all sizes and levels.

The professional staff of the Clinic come from a wide range of medical and mental health professions. All are members of multidisciplinary teams that take on individuals and families referred to the Clinic—the majority of referrals coming directly from local GPs. In addition, virtually everyone is engaged in the educational work of the institution, as well as in supervision and consultancy. The majority of staff have had prior experience working at senior level elsewhere in the NHS, in education, or in social services, and many have had direct professional experience of primary care in one or other capacity. Most staff do not work full-time at the Tavistock; rather, they work for part of every week in other agencies, including other NHS trusts, universities, or various clinical and training settings. In some cases, this includes private psychotherapy or psychoanalytic practice, and for a significant number it now also involves some kind of connection with primary care.

Because of the nature of the Clinic and its work, Tavistock therapists are familiar with working across a number of different boundaries. Most staff—including many of the contributors to this book—have a dual training and professional identity, both as members of a core discipline such as psychiatry or social work and as therapists. They are therefore used to using both of their professional hats at different times and are also willing to drop these hats and take on other roles as the occasion requires: including team leader, educational supervisor, group facilitator, or systems consultant. In addition, most are comfortable working simultaneously with both the inner, psychic world as this presents itself in clinical and organizational problems and with the outer, contextual realities that influence the genesis and development of such problems (Obholzer & Roberts, 1994). This approach is perhaps especially suited to settings such as primary health care, where the complex needs of patients and practitioners can defy reductionist attempts to impose a standardized way of thinking or working. In recent years, Tavistock staff, like everyone else working in the National Health Service, have had to embrace a vast range of new structures, terms, concepts, and practices. This includes such things as the new primary care organizations (PCOs), the care programme approach (CPA), clinical governance and audit, outcome research and evidence-based practice, and the National Service Frameworks. As the following chapters show, the kind of thinking offered by the Tavistock does not stand in opposition to these challenges. Instead, it can offer creative ways of rising to them, so that patients receive mental health services that are responsible at both the political and emotional level.

It would be a mistake to see the work of the Clinic as homogenous, or to identify a "Tavistock" style of working. Different practitioners draw on a variety of trainings, theoretical orientations, and professional experience in the way that they practice therapy or teach. It is certainly true that the dominant ethos of the Clinic is a psychoanalytic one, particularly drawing on object relations theory. This is reflected in the majority of recent publications by Tavistock staff (see, for example, Grier, 2004; Rhode & Klauber, 2004; Simpson & Miller, 2004). However, a minority of staff identify themselves as systemic psychotherapists (Papadopoulos & Byng Hall, 1997), while some would regard themselves as influenced by both schools of thought (Huffington, Armstrong, Halton, Hoyle, & Pooley, 2004). Similarly, the different departments—adult, adolescent, and child and family—have each developed distinctive ways of ways of approaching clinical problems or delivering training.

One thing certainly unites the work that takes place at the Tavistock: an implicit and explicit commitment to focused and sustained reflection on the whole range of work that comes within its orbit, drawing on psychotherapeutic insights and skills in order to inform that reflection. Indeed, one useful way of conceptualizing the Clinic's role might be as a "resource for reflection" within a health service and a wider culture that is for much of the time dominated by linear and concrete ways of thinking or by managerialism, and where time for focused and sustained reflection may be very restricted or even nonexistent. Such reflection may be a particularly precious resource for primary care workers, especially at a time like the present, when they seem to be beset with major problems of workload and morale, a plethora of government demands, and increasing public scrutiny.

The Tavistock and primary care

The Tavistock has always had strong links with front-line workers in the health and social services. It has always offered part-time "application trainings" for a variety of disciplines as wide ranging as social workers, teachers, counsellors, nurses, and police officers. There is a long history of connections with primary health care. The Clinic is perhaps best known in the field of primary care for the work of Michael Balint, and for the type of the case discussion seminars—so-called Balint groups—pioneered by him and his followers (Balint, 1957; Gosling & Turquet, 1964). Balint was the first person to conceptualize general practice explicitly as a form of therapy, to promote research into the GP consultation, and to advocate any form of clinical supervision in primary care. He had an acute understanding of the way that medical evangelism can often displace therapeutic engagement in primary care, and also of the potential for GPs to do valuable psychotherapeutic work of a kind that would be inadmissible for psychiatrists. Perhaps most importantly, he argued in favour of a coherent and seamless psychotherapy service that would unite GP training, educational supervision, case consultancy, and referral to secondary centres. This vision was powerfully supported by the medical director of the Tavistock at the time, John Sutherland (Sutherland, 1957).

In the decades since Balint worked at the Tavistock, the principles of his case discussion seminars have been taken up very widely in primary care, both nationally and internationally (E. Balint, Courtenay, Elder, Hull, & Julian, 1993). There are now very few formal Balint groups in existence—although one is still convened at the Tavistock—but Balint's ideas concerning the therapeutic nature of the consultation have become deeply influential in the training of GPs in Britain and elsewhere. In addition, Balint-style discussion groups have become widespread in vocational training course for GPs (Salinsky & Sackin, 2001). For a period of time in the 1970s, the Tavistock also followed up Balint and Sutherland's wider thinking by establishing attachments by psychologists, psychiatrists, and social workers to a few group practices in inner London (Graham & Sher, 1976; Sher, 1977). This innovation played a part in stimulating the growth of mental health "attachments" within primary care in many places in Britain—involving the employment of independent counsellors and therapists or on-site psychiatric "liaison" services in surgeries and health centres around the country (Sibbald, Addington-Hall, Brenneman, & Freeling, 1993).

The 1990s were a period of great upheaval in the NHS. The government began to promote the idea of a "primary-care-led NHS". In keeping with this idea, some GP practices were allowed for a time to become responsible for their own budgets. It became apparent that it would be helpful to have some practising GPs on the Tavistock Clinic staff itself, both for reasons of political prudence and, more importantly, to help to provide a more community-oriented service to patients. In 1995, two GPs with a special interest in psychotherapy were appointed part-time: Andrew Elder in the adult department and John Launer in the child and family department. They were given the role of promoting links with primary care, developing courses and events for GPs and primary care staff, and consulting to the institution generally concerning its relations with primary care. In 2001, Sue Blake took over Andrew Elder's role in the adult department.

Between them, the two staff GPs now offer wide-ranging input into many of the Clinic's activities, including both its professional trainings and its service development. This input, together with the further health service changes that have taken place, have led to an increased awareness in the Clinic of the needs of primary care and of how to meet them. On the educational side, the GPs have become involved in some of the core trainings for the different professions who attend the Tavistock. They have also set up a series of conferences on clinical supervision in primary care, and a multidisciplinary training for primary care based on ideas and skills from family therapy (Burton & Launer, 2003; Launer, 2002; Launer & Lindsey, 1997). Both of the staff GPs also function as therapists in their respective departments and as working members of the multidisciplinary clinical teams in the Clinic.

One of the most important roles of the Tavistock GPs has been the establishment of a regular primary care seminar, drawing together the staff members who now work in some capacity within primary care. The purpose of the seminar is to offer a space for therapists who are undertaking primary care work to reflect on it, to give them opportunities to share their understanding and expertise with each other, and to foster enthusiasm for this kind of work among other staff and trainees at the Clinic. This book has emerged in parallel with that seminar. It has been written by seminar members and gives an account of some of the work that its members do.

Psychotherapy: the challenge for primary care

The vast majority of mental health care in Britain takes place in GP surgeries and health centres. According to most estimates, a sizeable proportion of consultations in primary care—probably about one third—are largely or exclusively about psychological difficulties (Goldberg & Huxley, 1992). Similarly, about a fifth of all attenders are probably suffering from a formal mental disorder. As well as the serious mental disorders now covered by National Service Frameworks, primary care carries the immense burden of all the other manifestations of mental distress that can be equally disabling and enduring. If one considers, in addition, that most presentations of physical illness also have mental, emotional, or psychosocial dimensions, it is clear that GPs and their colleagues on the primary care team are by far the main mental health care professionals in the country.

The mental health case load in primary care is challenging in other ways too. Because primary care is accessible and not stigmatized socially, it attracts people with mental health problems who avoid or reject more formal care, including psychotherapy, even though they might benefit from it. Although conventional views of primary care include the idea that it mainly deals with those with trivial problems or essentially fulfils a "gatekeeping" role, the reality is quite different. The seriousness and complexity of cases seen in primary care can certainly rival that seen in any secondary or tertiary institution. Indeed, there is an "inverse care" law at work, which means that GPs, practice nurses, and health visitors often have to manage by themselves with the most complex and intractable cases because an onward referral is not practical or acceptable to these patients.

The primary care professionals who deal with this case load as a matter of routine do so with significant handicaps. There are the obvious limitations of the numbers of patients, consultation lengths, and adequate training in psychological treatment. In addition, many practitioners feel that their undergraduate and postgraduate education has failed to prepare them for the emotional demands of their work, in terms both of its scale and of its intensity (Burton & Launer, 2003). In marked contrast to the world of counselling and psychotherapy, systems of formal clinical supervision are almost entirely absent in the medical world, and even informal support systems may be lacking. In keeping with wider medical culture, tales of challenging cases may be exchanged in a competitive spirit rather than as an explicit means of seeking help. Indeed, the whole ethos of primary care is often quite unreflective in emotional terms, so that a premium is placed on working fast rather than sensitively, and on aiming for easily measurable targets—as reflected in physiological measurements or blood tests—rather than in subtler ends such as improved self-esteem or better personal and family relationships.

Most primary care practices and teams make very few referrals for psychotherapy, and some make none at all. Conversely, some psychotherapy departments receive most of their referrals from a relatively small number of enthusiastic local practitioners (who may themselves have had positive personal experiences of psychotherapy) or through internal referrals within the mental health care sector. The reasons for this are complex. There is widespread ignorance in primary care of the nature and uses of psychotherapy. There is a common belief that psychotherapy is only suitable for a narrow range of patients and conditions, or that all possible referrals for psychotherapy should first be seen by one of the more familiar professions such as mental health nurses, clinical psychologists, or psychiatrists. Practitioners who know a little about psychotherapy may assume that it only takes the form of intensive, long-term work. Others may be familiar with individual adult psychotherapy but know little or nothing about other areas, especially child psychotherapy and family therapy.

Many GPs and practice nurses—and even some health visitors and counsellors—see psychotherapy as a minor and peripheral speciality, or as a "super-speciality" analogous to neurosurgery or renal transplantation: in other words, as an area of medical activity that few of their patients will ever encounter, and that they do not need to engage with very closely. The idea that a psychotherapist might make a substantial contribution to a general practice or health centre would be a cause for puzzlement. (By contrast, the suggestion that someone with more obvious practical skills, like a physiotherapist or dermatologist, might join them regularly in the workplace would generally be celebrated.) There are, of course, practices that are notable exceptions in this respect, as the chapters in this book testify. However, it is worth making this point to draw attention to the fact that most people in primary care do not understand the potential that psychotherapy offers as a resource. Similarly, although there have been some adventurous attempts in some places to decentralize other mental health services into the community, there are few examples of free dialogue, constant collaboration, and sustained mutual learning between psychotherapy and primary care.

By contrast, one resource that is widely used for mental health problems in primary care is counselling. The nature and growth of primary care counselling have been very well documented (Bor & McCann, 1999; East, 1995; Keithley, Bond, & Marsh, 2002; Lees, 1999; Mellor-Clark, Simms-Ellis, & Burton, 2001; Wiener & Sher, 1998). In some ways the movement is a great success story, but in other ways it has been problematical. The public now has hugely greater access to "talking treatments" through their local surgery or health centre than ever before. At the same time, very few mental health workers in primary care have come from local NHS departments of psychotherapy. They generally do not have the support of multidisciplinary teams, nor the opportunities for cross-disciplinary supervision that are likely to be present in a psychotherapy department or CAMHS team. They may not be willing to do joint consultations with other professionals, and will almost certainly not do home visits. They are unlikely to have appropriate qualifications to work with parents of small infants, or with children, adolescents, and their families. A considerable number may not even have a formal qualification in either psychotherapy or counselling (Sibbald et al., 1993). There are many intelligent examples of individual counsellors and therapists working closely with GPs and learning a great deal about each others' work, but equally there are reports of boundary problems, including the isolation of counsellors from the rest of the primary care team, and misunderstandings over expectations and ground rules.

One challenge for primary care is to reconceptualize psycho-therapy as an approach that might benefit a huge range of patients. As examples later in this book show, this may include the worried mother who walks into a baby clinic to have her baby weighed, the adolescent who is showing the early signs of a preoccupation with eating, or the immigrant family who speak no English and are traumatized by the circumstances of their displacement. It encom-passes not only the whole range of cases that might normally be referred to other mental health professionals, but those who re-main with the GP because of the lack of adequate resources or the inflexibility of other agencies. These include frequent consulters, people given to persistent somatization, the isolated individuals who have barely any social contact beyond their surgery appoint-ments, and those who are struggling with the psychological conse-quences of physical illness, disability, or bereavement. And as these pages also show, psychotherapeutic services can be offered in languages other than English, or with the use of interpreters, or on home visits.

There are wider challenges for primary care too. One of these is to notice what it is often too painful to notice. As the procession of human distress parades daily before GPs and their primary care colleagues, it is only too easy for them to turn their gaze away from the sullen child whose parents have separated, or the husband who says "it's just one of those things" when his wife has died from multiple sclerosis, or the shaken victim of a road crash who turns up every month to ask for just one more certificate "and then I'm sure I'll be fine". The presence of a psychotherapist, and of psycho-therapeutic thinking, can embolden practitioners to identify and reach out to such people, in the knowledge that more support might be available both for the patients and for themselves.

To accept psychotherapeutic help within a practice—at any level beyond the most conventional model of liaison work—is of course to accept that practitioners in primary care have great emotional needs too. For any psychotherapeutic attachment to work well, there needs to be a willingness in at least some of the doctors and nurses to reflect on the dynamics of interactions with patients and families, and on the almost universal presence in primary care of the processes that impede or contaminate help: these include collusion, denial, alienation, moralization, and rationalization. There needs to be a willingness to reflect honestly on what is going on in the thoughts and feelings of the consulting doctor or nurse as well the patient. Practitioners need to see the patient–doctor or patient–nurse relationship as the focus for work as much as the "case". They may also need to consider how interactions within the team can echo or amplify the difficulties that patients have brought.

Taking on a psychotherapist involves more than taking just one new person into the practice or team. It involves acknowledging in some form that the thinking, working practices, and culture of primary care themselves need help. GPs and primary care nurses who find the courage to enlist psychotherapeutic help are in some sense accepting that there is scope for more thoughtfulness, more sensitivity, and more openness in the work that they do. They are accepting a challenge to their own inevitable tendencies to automatism and, in some cases, their paternalism. They are accepting that the demands they face in their daily work can take a great toll on the lives and mental health of practitioners themselves. They are recognizing that primary care itself may be in need of a "talking cure".

Primary care: the challenge for psychotherapy

Psychotherapists who encounter the world of primary care can react in a number of ways. One form of response is no doubt avoidant: some have only ever seen primary care as patients themselves, or may have had only brief and bruising professional contacts with GPs, and in consequence they may see it as "the work setting from hell". They find it impossible to imagine that the kind of work they do as therapists could ever take place amid such frenzy, or in the presence of what they see as a widespread culture of psychological distancing or denial. They may be deterred by the business ethos of primary care, or by the way that biomedical and behavioural ways of understanding mental distress are dominant in many primary care settings.

Other psychotherapists see primary care in a more positive light, but mainly in terms of being a fruitful hunting ground for referrals for formal psychotherapy rather than for its wider potential. They may identify a mission to "rescue" GPs by persuading them about the possible benefits of psychotherapy for their patients, or they may become focused on the possibility that an increased number of referrals might save their psychotherapy departments or enhance their own practices. Either way, they see their principal task in relation to primary care as an educational one, helping GPs and others to detect appropriate cases that might benefit from psychotherapeutic input, either through referral or by having a therapist doing sessional work on site.

Like an increasing number of therapists nowadays, the contributors to this book all take a far wider view of the possibilities that primary care can offer psychotherapy—and of the challenges it presents them with as a profession. They all recognize that primary care offers unmatched opportunities for working equitably across the whole life cycle, with the kinds of clientele and the kinds of problems that would never reach more protected settings such as the NHS psychotherapy department. For example, they have discovered that they are able to deliver psychotherapy services across a wider social spectrum, or to a greater range of ethnic groups, or to particularly deprived populations such as refugees, or simply to the kinds of patients or families who—for various reasons—might never otherwise entertain the possibility of therapeutic help. As the following chapters show, work in primary care can also provide many learning opportunities for therapists. It can give them an eye-opening perspective on the social and epidemiological contexts from which their normal caseload arises. It can help them to appreciate that the patients who reach psychotherapy outpatient departments are not necessarily the most challenging, nor indeed the most needy, that might be seen. They learn that social and organizational factors often determine that very many people who might be helped never get referred on account of arbitrary reasons, often connected with various kinds of prejudice or discrimination.

As a result of their exposure, therapists coming into primary care are inevitably challenged to reconsider some of their own cherished beliefs concerning their own theoretical frameworks, their ways of working in the consulting-room, and their views of their own roles. For example, rigid rules about consultation length or frequency may make little sense when seeing the kinds of patients that they are likely to come across in primary care, especially those suffering from multiple material and social deprivations. Many therapists find themselves becoming far more flexible in their willingness to see people sporadically, or at long and unpredictable intervals, or in less than ideal physical circumstances, while still recognizing that they are offering a legitimate form of therapy. They may move away from a belief that a course of "treatment" must lay a problem to rest for ever, and instead feel more comfortable with the notion that therapy may have an important place in helping people to manage small but necessary changes at certain difficult moments in the life cycle. In many ways, the challenge for therapists is to discover how to learn from GPs and primary care nurses to function in the more informal way of these disciplines without becoming so similar as to lose their distinctive strengths and effectiveness as therapists.

Depending on the quality and interest of the practice concerned, many therapists who enter primary care discover an enhanced respect for the mental health work that doctors and nurses do every day. They may be surprised by what primary care practitioners manage to achieve in astonishingly small bursts of time, or under adverse conditions. Rather than seeing such work as amateur or substandard psychotherapy, they gain an understanding of primary care as a milieu where a kind of therapy takes place in its own right. It is a form of therapy that has been termed "ultra-brief, ultra-long therapy" (Launer, 1996). In other words, although each episode might last only a few minutes, the therapeutic relationship itself may continue over several generations and be imbued with a great depth of mutual trust. Such therapy, delivered very widely in primary care, may have an important part to play in the overall system of mental health care for the population.

One area where many psychotherapists learn to review their prior beliefs in the context of primary care is in relation to confidentiality (Waskett, 1999). Working within a complex network of staff who share care for the patients—and who have continuing legal responsibility for them even while they are seeing a therapist— means that therapists have to give a great deal of thought to the extent of confidentiality required in this setting, and they may decide that this has to be far more negotiable than would normally be the case. In a working milieu where many people may need to know about patients who are at risk of self-harm, or of violence to others including health care staff, therapists may need to subscribe to a code of "confidentiality within the team" rather than the more purist code of the "secure frame" (Hoag, 1992; Launer, 1994a). They may need to find a balanced position that allows openness to information-sharing without being drawn into gossip or into collusion with intrusive referrers.

Perhaps the biggest challenge facing therapists who enter primary care concerns the need to work with the consulting context as much as with the content of cases. Therapists, especially those who work privately for a great deal of the time, may be used to a physical working context that is so neutral that it is rendered almost invisible. In primary care, they will encounter the exact opposite—a complex, highly populated, sharply conspicuous network of disciplines, personalities, and interconnected human systems. As many have found, thoughtful work of any kind with patients can only be done when an adequate amount of thoughtful work has been done with the referring network. Therapists need to be able to think creatively about, and work tactfully with, such issues as power relations, interdisciplinary rivalries, and political and financial pressures. They need to be alert to practice politics and work tactfully around them.

For all these reasons, many therapists find themselves in some way letting go some of the clear boundaries they may hitherto have assumed to have existed between assessment, clinical work, supervision, consultancy, collaborative work, and training. They may, for instance, find that the working context in primary care demands that they spend as much—or more—time in case discussion with referrers than they do on the cases themselves. They may become drawn—and willing to be drawn—into helping the practice or team with wider issues concerning its own function. In time, some therapists come to reassess the nature of their role as a result of their primary care experiences, so that they see it less in terms of treating patients and more in terms of holding on to the faculty for reflection. This is a faculty that is often desperately needed in primary care. If offered thoughtfully, it may be much appreciated.

The contributions to this book

The authors of this book come from a variety of different professions and have a range of different interests, but all are trained as psychotherapists. Some are individual adult or child psychotherapists, working with a psychodynamic perspective. Others are systemic family therapists. Nearly all the writers are from among the more senior and experienced practitioners in the Clinic, reflecting the seriousness and difficulty of work in primary care. A few do not currently work with the Clinic but are closely associated with it through their original training or as former staff members. A sizeable proportion of the work described is with infants, children, and their families, reflecting the predominant workload and training interests of the Clinic itself. Several chapters include a focus on working with immigrants and refugees, particularly those from Bangladesh. This reflects the demography of those areas mainly served by the Clinic, the considerable mental health needs of these populations, and the obligation we feel to develop appropriate services and models of working for them.

The settings for the primary care attachments are wide-ranging. They include traditional GP practices in a number of different localities, a health centre, a health visiting team, and a community centre. Some of the work has arisen directly out of the Clinic's recent drive to raise the profile of primary care attachments, while others are describing work that they have initiated independently. Each attachment clearly has its own style, deriving from the interests of the clinicians and the needs of the practice or team. The "life cycle" of the attachments also varies greatly—for example, some of the work has been carried out over more than two decades, while other therapists have gone into the primary care setting for a defined project over a limited period of time.

The attachments themselves cover a spectrum of activity, from purely clinical work to supervision, facilitation of case discussion, joint consultation on some cases, and wider consultative and developmental work. There are considerable differences between contributors in terms of their theoretical and practical approaches. However, all share a commitment to learning how to think and work differently in the primary care setting. They have all found ways of adapting their ideas and techniques to fit in with the particular nature of primary care, as well as promoting more reflective thinking in primary care practitioners themselves. Like most therapists who enter this setting, the authors of this book have found that there may be no single theoretical model that can make sense of primary care work and no single working methodology that will by itself be helpful. Rather than being an attempt to prescribe a "one-size-fits-all" model for psychotherapeutic work in primary care, the chapters that follow represent the diverse and constantly evolving nature of the work that the Clinic offers.

Finally, a note on terminology. We use the term "primary care" to mean GPs and those professions who commonly work alongside them, including health visitors, practice nurses, community nurses, and practice counsellors. We also use it to embrace mental health initiatives in the community, such as Sure Start. As far as the words "psychotherapist" and "therapist" are concerned, when applied to the editors and authors of this book, they mean exactly what they say: namely, that we are all trained and qualified adult, child, or family psychotherapists, registered with the British Confederation of Psychotherapists or the United Kingdom Council for Psychotherapy. In other contexts in this book—which should be fairly obvious when they occur—we use the words as a convenient shorthand to mean any mental health professional with a psychotherapeutic orientation. This may include counsellors, mental health nurses, clinical psychologists, and psychiatrists, among others. We would not want any clinician to feel excluded from a sense of community with the writers of this book if they share our interest in working at the interface with primary care in a way that is informed by psychotherapeutic ideas.

CHAPTER TWO

A child psychotherapist in the baby clinic of a general practice: standing by the weighing scales thirty years on

Dilys Daws

Just over thirty years ago I started work at the baby clinic of a GP practice: the James Wigg Practice in Kentish Town, London. I called my first paper on work there "Standing by the weighing scales" (Daws, 1985). I am gratified that this phase has caught on with some of my colleagues, and I hear them jokingly say, "This is standing by the weighing scales kind of work" when they talk about their ventures into various settings. I wrote then about the difficulties of doing this work, and even though the practice I visit is friendly and welcoming, of feeling exposed and vulnerable in an institution not one's own. When asked now about the qualities needed, I usually say: "a very thick skin"!

Why am I still there thirty years later? As a psychotherapist I look at patients' present situations in terms of early experience. In the same way, my own interest in working as a child psychotherapist in general practice must have its roots in family experience. My

An earlier version of this chapter was published as a paper in *Clinical Child Psychology and Psychiatry* (1999) 4: 9–22.

father, Jack Kahn, before training as a psychiatrist, was a GP in Huddersfield in the days when practices were run from the doctor's home. My mother answered the telephone, helped do the accounts, and knew who all the patients were. Today she would be called the practice manager. As we grew up, my sister and I saw the exhaustion and frustration of this life, but what remains in the memory is the excitement, the essential nature of the work, and the close contacts with the local community. In addition, my father was a town councillor; for some years chairman of the health committee. Huddersfield, in Yorkshire, was a wool-manufacturing town that prided itself on its public health standards; the legend was that Huddersfield was the first to have achieved *general* vaccination in the nineteenth century. Before the NHS, working-men paid a few pence a week to be "on the panel" and be able to be seen by a GP, but this did not include their wives and children. My father, like many doctors, saw these families for no fee. His income came from his (modestly) fee-paying patients. So doctors themselves were running an informal balancing system. This was realistic for those like my father, working in districts where there were also lower-middle- and middle-class patients—not possible in more poverty-stricken areas. So by the time my father left general practice in 1947, I had absorbed the idea that public policies and individual commitment could jointly be powerful forces in preventative health measures.

With the creation of the National Health Service in 1948, the shape of general practice changed greatly. The family doctor charter of 1966 encouraged large group practices; some were set up in specially designed health centres. Multidisciplinary primary care teams developed, including health visitors, practice nurses, and others. Various medical specialists became attached to or visited large general practices. In recent years this has coincided with a movement from within mental health services to go out into the community.

As the introduction to this book makes clear, the Tavistock Clinic was at the forefront of this development. Following Balint's pioneering work there was much further study of the essential nature of the therapeutic ingredients of what goes on between doctor and patient, notably by his wife, Enid Balint, and her colleagues (Balint & Norrell, 1973; Balint et al., 1993; M. Balint, 1957). Alexis Brook, who was one of the pioneers in visiting a general practice, trained others, including myself, to help GPs "increase their skills in identifying and tackling the psychological problems they meet in daily life" (Brook, 1978).

General practitioners have to diagnose, and manage in some way, frankly psychiatric disorders. They also have to deal with the more nebulous connections between physical symptoms and states of mind. Launer (1994a) has made a valuable differentiation between the doctor's use of emotional insights in his day to day work with patients, leading into "opportunistic" counselling, contrasting this with formal prearranged counselling either by the GP or by a designated counsellor. He humorously uses the term "little C" and "big C" to refer to these. Zalidis (1994), another general practitioner, wrote: "When a patient feels unwell he or she may present to the general practitioner with symptoms which can be the physical accompaniments of anxiety, or with anxiety that is precipitated by physical symptoms, or a combination of both" (p. 180). The emotional consequences of physical illness and, even more so, the psychic underpinning of many somatic states have been increasingly recognized in general practice. Similarly, Elder (1986) has described the doctor's support at periods when patients are experiencing life events,

> that are some of the psychological determinants of people's lives. . . . Morbidity and presentations to the doctor are known to increase when people are negotiating their major transitions of life, or life events. This means that the doctor is often involved when psychic history is being made. He can, therefore, influence this process a little, for better or for worse. [p. 75]

A child psychotherapist in the baby clinic

Until recently, counselling and psychotherapy in general practice has mainly been with adults. As in other mental health services, children's needs have been less well recognized. However, the practice in which I work puts children and their families high on the agenda. My connection with the practice is through the baby clinic (Daws, 1995). In the United Kingdom, these clinics are universally available to families with children from birth up to five years. They are staffed by health visitors who are nurses with an additional training and qualification, and also by doctors. The clinics have a statutory function in providing immunizations and routine developmental checks as well as a more informal setting where parents can get advice and support on their infant's progress. In the practice that I visit, two counsellors work with adult patients, and we keep in touch about referrals that might overlap. So I am discussing my consultative role from a personal stance; my colleagues fulfil similar functions.

Since I first visited the practice, I have been going there one morning a week, at a time when a baby clinic is being held. For many young parents the baby clinic is a crucial institution, for some even a life-line. The clinic is equally important for the professionals as the focused time of the week in which they see and discuss the infants they are responsible for. By being present during the clinic, I can also, to some extent, be part of its routine and be available to talk about families that doctors and health visitors have on their minds. The development of this work reflects the recent world-wide interest in parent–infant psychotherapy and its applications.

Work in a baby clinic enables families to get help with their infant's development as early as possible; the hope is that later difficulties in the relationship between parents and child may thus be forestalled (Fonagy, 1998). Serious disturbances of feeding and sleeping, crying and difficulty in bonding continuously confront doctors and health visitors. Many of these can be helped by routine primary care work, but when problems persist, they may be referred to me. It is striking that in this brief work with distressed families large numbers of parents have anxieties about separation and most have experienced traumatic bereavement or loss (Daws, 1993).

Although this work is brief, often one or two meetings only, the method is psychoanalytically based. Problems are thought of as connected with emotions and in the context of the baby's and the parents' history. I ask parents to tell me the problem but then add that in order to help them, I need to understand how the problem has arisen. I ask them for memories of the pregnancy and birth and of how they got together. This may lead on to talking about their own childhoods and their relationship to their parents now. In describing all this, links between ideas often emerge, and parents seem strikingly relieved to make these connections.

Psychosomatic aspects of the work

Doctors and health visitors in the community are struggling every day with body–mind issues. As a psychoanalytically trained worker I hope to help in understanding the emotional meaning of some patients' symptoms and the feelings aroused in professionals by patients. In families, thoughts about normal development of infants and parents' care is directed first to the baby's *body* and to physical needs. A parent's first duty is simply to keep their baby alive. Stern (1985) has described the interplay between babies and their caretakers and noted that babies need another person in order to experience their own bodies. Babies need the physical mediation of another person to satisfy their hunger or deal with other physical states, such as getting to sleep. Stern says: "others regulate the infant's experience of somatic state . . . in all such regulations a dramatic shift in neurophysiological state is involved" (p. 103).

In a baby clinic, babies' bodies are examined, as well as attention paid to development and relationships. The weighing scales are important as a focal point for the baby clinic (Daws, 1985). The rationale for parents coming to the clinic can be to have their baby weighed. The baby's body is looked at, appreciated, and measured by parents and professionals. Also apparent is the quality of the mother's ability to protect her infant. Babies are vulnerable in their nakedness when put on the weighing scale and picked up again. We all know the infants' startle reaction when their clothes are taken off. Small babies can look as though they feel they are "falling to pieces" at this moment. Many mothers intuitively sense this and wrap their baby round by holding with their gaze and with their voice, as well as with their hands. Others cannot do so, and the baby's vulnerability is exposed. All this can be noticed by a receptive health visitor and help her think about what a particular family needs from her. (Incidentally, it is worth noting that an adult, undressing to be examined by the doctor, may be as liable to the startle reaction as any infant.) The weighing scales themselves can also be seen as a kind of "scales of justice". This can be a benign process when babies are doing well. However, when there are serious concerns, parents who feel persecuted may split off their own judgement and argue about the accuracy of the scales, leaving professionals alone to worry about the infant's needs. With infants who are failing to thrive, this can be a real danger.

It takes as much skill to stand next to a weighing machine as it does not to talk during a psychotherapy session! The skill of thinking on behalf of the patient is only evident if one says one's thoughts in words; but if one talks too much, reflective thought has no time to grow. Standing doing nothing equally requires skill if it is not to be puzzling and persecuting to the people around. It is legitimized in a busy clinic because all professionals stand at times looking around, sometimes deciding what to do next, sometimes talking to one another. I could be any of these: standing to watch what is going on, or ready for discussion. I must be careful not to get annoyingly in the way of busy staff actually trying to weigh the babies or get to the filing cabinet! If I am too self-contained, it must seem that my observations are for some unexplained private use: if I look too efficiently outgoing, mothers hand me their baby books to check them into the clinic! By watching, I gain what for me is invaluable—seeing a whole range of mothers and babies interact. The time I spend is, of course, usually a few minutes here and there, between sessions with patients, perhaps longer when families fail to turn up. Weekly, my store of impressions of normality and pathology is reinforced, so that when someone is referred to me with a problem, I have a background of knowing where this might fit in with what usually happens between parents and babies.

The families who are referred with their baby are often those who seem to remain in a high state of anxiety, in spite of a great deal of supportive work by primary care professionals. There is usually an actual symptom in the baby, such as a feeding or a sleep problem. Often we then find relationship issues between parents and baby, such as separation problems, perhaps based on earlier bereavements and losses. Some people talk more easily about physical symptoms than about emotions, and McDougall (1986) has popularized the concept of alexythymia (Nemiah & Sifneos, 1970) of people unable to recognize and distinguish their emotions. Parents, in this state of mind, do not *name* their children's emotions, and the children are likely to express feelings through bodily sensations, experiencing physical rather than mental discomfort. Whatever the origin, we must not forget that there has actually been a physical symptom. The baby has *actually* cried with colic, been unable to sleep, is feeding too often, or failing to thrive. Our bodies and minds intertwine; and it does sometimes seem that babies' bodies are affected by the anxieties and traumas in their parents' minds.

A psychoanalytic approach

In this style of work emotions, relationships, and personal histories are all taken as relevant in thinking about an infant's problem. This is different from the focus of some other therapists working behaviourally or cognitively. Douglas and Richman (1984), for example, state:

> In practice we have found that generally it is not useful to delve back into the past, or into the parents' or the child's psyche to find out the cause of a sleep problem. It is more profitable to concentrate on the here and now of how parents are responding at night-time and how that might affect the sleep patterns. [p. 47]

By contrast, in my own experience, when families are really listened to, even in brief work, it may enable them to feel that something crucial about them has been understood. They may then be better able to understand and respond to each other and thus deal with their children's problems (Daws, 1993).

Observation and consultation

The child psychotherapist's training begins with the experience of infant observation—seeing an "ordinary" baby at home, with mother and perhaps other members of the family, for an hour a week for two years (Miller, Rustin, Rustin, & Shuttleworth, 1989). The trainee has the chance to see the normal physical, emotional, and social development of an infant. Trainees can also experience the emotions stirred up by this exposure to the intensity of being with a tiny baby, and the drama of the mother–baby relationship.

Learning to observe, with respect and with self-containment, is a difficult art. It is also an economical way of learning how to start being a therapist, how to observe what is going on for others in an emotionally heightened situation; to note the feelings stirred up in oneself, to learn how to manage them, and to use these as a source of information, *not* as a key to action. This observing stance is the basis for the consultation that is part of what I as a child psychotherapist can offer the baby clinic.

At the end of the baby clinic, a meeting of health visitors, doctors, and the nurse who has carried out immunizations reviews each attendance, and any worries about a baby and its family are noted. These meetings are a necessary exchange of information; they are also an opportunity to share the experience of the anxieties that have accumulated during the two hours or more of the baby clinic. By being there, I can thus be part of the process where anxieties are picked up and highlighted, or where the group reassures itself that all can be left and reconsidered again next week.

One of my problems is to decide when it is appropriate to help *raise* the anxiety level in colleagues and when to help *settle* it. In general practice, and in the baby clinic, doctors and health visitors are seeing the whole range of the population. In the main they are supporting normality and healthy development. In order for such a clinic to survive, there must be a basic assumption that the anxieties brought constantly are being met, and dealt with, by the routine activities of the clinic.

Parents who have just had a baby are *normally* in a heightened state of emotion: life and death feelings are part of the ordinary state of a baby clinic. Doctors and health visitors have to tolerate the stress of this and evaluate when some of it is out of the ordinary and needs special attention. My focus on anxieties can be a relief to the team, but at other times it can be irritating, and I am felt to pathologize ordinary life events. The professionals also have to cope with the feelings aroused in themselves. This leads to what may be the most helpful contribution that a psychoanalytically trained worker can bring to a primary care team: helping the team to learn to identify the feelings aroused by patients, to manage these feelings, and indeed to use them as a valuable source of information about feelings the patient might have and be unable to tolerate.

Meetings with general practice registrars

As part of this process there are regular meetings with the GP registrars—doctors in a trainee year. One of the skills of a GP is in assessing what lies behind a patient's request for attention to a particular symptom or condition: "It's my leg, doctor." Any illness or symptom implies subtle connections between body and mind. Many patients are longing to be asked about themselves and have a need to be "known" by their doctor; others are offended by any straying from the obvious task. In this practice the registrars are well supported by their trainers, but cumulative experience of patients' undefined needs can be overwhelming. One registrar said to me that the meetings were a chance to "let off steam". This, in itself, must be useful for a profession that has a high sickness rate (Hale & Hudson, 1992).

In an inner-city practice there are patients who seem to bring generations of social, relationship, and personal problems to any consultation. When small children from such a family are brought to the surgery, it feels like the opportunity for a "fresh start". Young idealistic doctors bring energy to this. They also wish to be realistic, and expectations of what is possible need to be thought about. Airing the feelings of hope, talking of therapeutic zeal and of disappointment, makes it possible to keep on trying. Doctors need to learn to entrust such feelings to each other; on occasion the visiting psychotherapist, by virtue of being an outsider, can be the useful recipient of these feelings. It is, of course, not appropriate for these exchanges to lapse into personal psychotherapy sessions; they must be confined to the medical task. Doctors, whether in training or experienced, have to learn to work fast. Corney (1996) has pointed out that doctors do not "have the luxury of time to reflect on their practice". Any psychotherapist working with GPs learns to speed up and report back fast! However, it may be that, as Corney suggests, "if doctors took more time for reflection, it could enable them to function more effectively and feel more supported" (p. 137).

Meetings with health visitors

I also have regular meetings with the health visitors in addition to many short informal discussions during baby clinics. We sometimes talk about cases they might wish to refer to me. More often, we will talk about a case that is perplexing or, even more likely, irritating or angering them. We talk about where these feelings come from, about how some people provoke anger and rejection as they go through life. A health visitor who understands that the parent may be re-enacting the rejection she has experienced in her childhood will not be put off. The mother may start to feel understood and supported for the first time and may, in turn, manage the baby's feelings better.

I may be able to back the health visitor in keeping going with the parents who need this help most but turn it away. Because they are available to *all* families of new babies, health visitors are able to support families through the uncertain first days of getting to know a new baby, and how to care for it. When health visitors give expert advice to families, it may also feel as though they are symbolically "parenting" these families, especially when there is a lack of such support. The beneficial effect of this is unquantifiable. When families are in emotional trouble, the health visitor, who already has a relationship built on many meetings and much knowledge, is in the best position to help. This implies case loads that allow time to work with the families that do need more attention, rather than having to refer them on to designated specialist health visitors dealing only with identified problems or to other professionals.

Postnatal depression

In this practice, general practitioners and health visitors alike have always been sensitive to the emotional state of women who have recently had babies, but postnatal depression is a condition that is difficult to diagnose. First, most women feel *really* depressed only when alone with their babies. In the presence, even briefly, of an interested health visitor they may feel cared for. On the other hand, those who are most severely depressed can be so flat, elusive, and dismissing of any approach that it is easy for the health visitor to feel unwanted and, in turn, not be readily available for the mother.

Cox's study on postnatal depression included giving a brief questionnaire on their emotional state to women who had just given birth (Cox, Holden, & Sagovsky, 1987). This Edinburgh Post-natal Depression Scale is effective in detecting depression, but its use is still controversial. Some of the most clinically inspired health visitors feel that the discovery of the depression through the scale creates a barrier between themselves and the mother, and that the real discovery of depression needs to take place during a spontane-ous, open-ended conversation between health visitor and mother. The questionnaire can then be used to back up clinical intuition, and Seeley (2001) says that the scale is only as good as the person interpreting it. Timing and context are thus crucial in sensitive use of the scale. However, the Edinburgh scale did alert us to the prevalence of postnatal depression. Following this, Holden and colleagues suggested that eight weekly counselling sessions by a health visitor is an effective way of helping postnatally depressed women (Holden, Sagovsky, & Cox, 1989). This is an important advance in treatment and underlines the crucial part that health visitors play in the primary care facilities of this country.

The counselling function
of general practitioners and health visitors

I believe that one of my most helpful functions is to back the primary care team to be "braver" in taking on the difficulties in relationships that many families have. The long-term relationship families can have with their GP and health visitor is in itself a model for parents. Referrals to specialists (including myself) must be carefully considered lest they puncture this attachment.

How, therefore, does a health visitor or a general practitioner who has such a long-term relationship with an individual or a family do some serious "counselling" work and then go back to the usual brief consultations? The latter are captured in the title of the book *Six Minutes for the Patient* (Balint & Norrell, 1973), the authors of which describe the brief, intense, and close contact, which they call a "flash", that can happen even within an ordinary consulta-tion between doctor and patient. Such a meeting may lead to an offer of a longer appointment, which has more of the nature of a counselling session. I believe that through just one, or perhaps a few, such meetings, a patient can feel that they are really known about by their doctor or health visitor and that this remains a reference point when the more routine relationship is resumed. It is important that this process does remain under control, otherwise the general practitioner's constant fear of endless need becoming unleashed could become a reality.

So, how much can, or should, health visitors and general practitioners themselves take part in counselling? Professionals, even without a psychotherapy or counselling training, can extend their scope of working. Zalidis (1994) describes a contained way in which doctors can look at the here and now relationship with their patients:

> The doctor's increased understanding of the relationship with his patients enables him to become more tolerant and more receptive to what his patients are telling him, without necessarily attempting to challenge their defences, or make interpretations. The resulting improved relationship with the doctor can lead to a therapeutic change in the patient. [p. 182]

Elder (1987) has pointed out the emotional dangers of attempting too much. He says that general practitioners

> hoping to make their patients better will soon be exhausted and disillusioned. Doctors in general practice have to learn to live with their patients in a much more unchanging world than often both would wish. The frustrations of this has to be borne, just as uncertainty also has to be, in order to allow other possible changes to occur. [p. 54]

He asks to what extent to these two worlds—the doctor's and the patient's—meet in moments of understanding.

The key to understanding is *listening,* and there are two elements to this: first, listening to patients, giving them time for what they have to say, and taking note of how they say it; second, attending to the feelings stirred up in oneself as a worker and seeing what information these feelings bring to bear on the patient. This approach can be taught by working jointly with a referring professional. For example, I saw a mother with two hyperactive toddlers, together with their health visitor. Hyperactivity, like many other presenting problems, may be a sign of a relationship difficulty; it is necessary first to hear in detail about the nature of the problem. The mother told us how out of control she experienced her two boys. It also became evident that she was very angry with them for this behaviour, and she rarely looked at them as she spoke. It is important not to go directly to solutions of the symptom. In talking with this mother, we soon heard a story of losses in her life, and it seemed that she had been severely postnatally depressed and was still suffering from depression. She cried as she told her story, and the health visitor put her arm around her. The two children quietened down as they played, seeming relieved that their mother had had a chance to unburden herself, possibly for the first time. Perhaps they perceived us as looking after her and could relax their "responsibility" for her. She was able to think about whether her children's "hyperactive" rushing about was their attempt to produce some life in their flat, dispirited mother (Murray & Cooper, 1997). As she began to feel sympathetic to their predicament, she was able to watch their play, and the children, in turn, responded to this interest, showing her the small toy cars and animals they were using.

Afterwards, the health visitor told me that she was impressed with how much the mother had been able to confide in us. Then she confessed: "At first I couldn't stand the silences". I thought, "What silences?" Compared to a psychotherapy session, it had been all talk! In order to communicate emotions as well as thoughts, we have to use more than just words. All sorts of nonverbal signs pass from one person to another, and some silences may be an essential part of this.

Silences are necessary, but long ones are to be avoided: a few seconds may be enough. What is important is for the patient sometimes to be the one to break the silence. Psychoanalytic method is based on *free association*—that is, patients letting their minds move freely from one thought to another, to see where thoughts lead. It would be pretentious and confusing to use this method in ordinary professional exchanges. Patients naturally expect a conversation. But it can be very rewarding to allow patients the space sometimes to say what comes into *their* minds, following what *they* have just said, rather than workers breaking the train of thought with their own words.

Working like this is difficult because much of what we say to patients can be to keep them quiet, to *stop* the flow of what they might say next, especially if they are depressed or disturbed in some way. For example, postnatally depressed mothers may, given the chance, relate shocking thoughts of anxiety, anger, self-hatred, hatred of the baby or partner, disturbing dreams, fears of damage that has, or might, happen. The urge to cheer people up or to keep things under control rather than to hear the content of depressing or upsetting thoughts can be overwhelming. So anyone who extends their range of competence, becoming more of a counsellor, needs *supervision* as they get to grips with what happens when patients are encouraged to talk. McLeod (1988) has emphasized the need for supervision for all counsellors, and Corney (1993) has pointed out that training improves outcome.

Clinical applications

In the baby clinic, where does the need for specific clinical work by the psychotherapist fit in? There are various reasons why a referral may be justified. First, there are some parents who can make use of intensive time away from the known primary care workers when issues can be explored in depth. This is separate protected time with some privacy, though not necessarily confidential from the referrer.

The referral process itself, where the GP or health visitor suggests to the family that they could see a psychotherapist, can feel either like concerned care or as a rejection. I treasure a remark made by one GP about a too-hasty referral to me by a colleague, saying that the patient had been "mugged" by the therapy!

Next are the cases where anxiety remains after medical needs have been properly attended to. In one referral the mother of a 6-week-old baby told me that she had called out four doctors over the weekend because the baby had a cold. Each doctor had suggested to her that she should see me. They had all sensed her anxiety level, but it turned out that this anxiety had a very real basis. She had had various losses and traumas, including a stillbirth. Any small ailment triggered fears of serious loss. In such a case, putting a patient's fears into words is, of course, helpful in itself, and going through an actual traumatic experience may help recovery from it; the work also needs to take on the personal meaning for an individual of such events. Any parent will naturally have ambivalent feelings towards their baby. When the baby is especially precious, it can be hard to own the hostile part of these feelings. Unacknowledged ambivalence can be one of the clues to excessive anxiety. A therapist who can bear hearing painful experiences and thoughts that the patient feels to be shocking may help anxiety move to a more manageable level.

Paradoxically, it can sometimes be useful to see families even when there are many problems besetting them, and it would appear that there is too much going on for psychotherapy in itself to be effective. Meeting the family face to face does at least give me a vivid experience of their problems and of the effect a "heart-sink" family can have on a would-be helpful professional. I can then share the feelings of the primary care team as we discuss how to manage such long-term difficult families. It can also be realistic to use specialist time to attempt to reach, in the familiar surroundings of their health centre, a few families not normally thought likely to use this work. The attempt in itself stretches my technique; it may help some deprived people to feel that their doctor and health visitor have not given up on them, and might stir them into more self-awareness and responsibility. I often think that if all referrals were "suitable cases for treatment", we would all be missing an opportunity to see who might be able to use the chance to think differently about themselves.

Case study: "Harry"

I now give a brief example of a case where the symptom in the baby could be seen to connect with experiences in the family. A family was referred for a severe sleep problem in their 9-month-old baby, Harry.

When I met the family, father, mother, and baby all gazed at me seriously as I invited them into the consulting-room. The parents relaxed as we made our introductions. I remarked that the baby looked worried. Father said that he was usually a smiley baby. I said that perhaps they were all a bit worried about coming to talk about problems with a strange person, and that it showed how sensitive he was to their feelings. Both parents agreed. By commenting at the start on the level of anxiety that seemed apparent to me, I was setting the scene for a focus on emotional issues in the consultation.

With this clue of the baby's sensitivity, I was first told about the presenting problem: that this baby could only go to sleep while on the breast, and that he woke many times during the night and each time had to be fed back to sleep by his mother. During the day he did not need to be fed so much but was very distressed if his mother was out of his sight.

I then asked about the pregnancy and birth and of the process of getting together in the early weeks. As the story unfolded, I asked about the parents' own childhoods and tried to make links. In this family, one piece of information was overwhelming. There had been a traumatic event at the birth of the baby: at the end of labour, the mother had suffered an amniotic fluid embolism and had become unconscious. There was then a night of endeavour to save her life, and she was told that if a particular consultant who recognized her serious condition had not happened to be there, she might well have died. She told me of this doctor calling her name as she recovered consciousness—it felt as though he was calling her back to life.

As I considered this dramatic story, the parents told me more about the baby's waking during the night. They also had a 9-year-old son, who, they felt, had no problems. I also learnt that the mother's parents had both died when she was in her adolescence. I remarked that she knew how unbearable it was to lose a parent, and perhaps she needed to keep her baby especially close to her, when he had also so nearly lost her. Many cases of severe sleep problems have had a serious loss in the family's history (Daws, 1993). It seemed clear that her anxiety was also communicating itself to the baby in a way that prevented him from switching off into sleep.

I then happened to ask her whether she had nightmares about her near-death. She said that she had not, and that she herself barely slept. It occurred to me that her experience of being called back to life by the doctor had made her equate sleep with death. It sounded as though she had to stay awake so as not to lapse into death. She agreed, but then told me that her difficulty in sleeping dated from her father's death. He had died of a heart-attack, and she had found him dead in bed in the morning. She had always felt that if she had woken earlier and gone to him sooner, he would not have died. When her mother had died a few years later, she became responsible for younger siblings and similarly felt that she had to stay "on guard" on their behalf. This mother's own difficulty in sleeping is, therefore, multiply determined.

I next discovered that father had a different approach to sleep. Although a committed and involved father, he could not help his wife with the night-time problems, as he slept so deeply that he did not wake when the baby cried. It then emerged that his own mother had never woken to attend to him as a baby, his father having been the one to respond. Here again we see evidence of the impact of attachment relationships on sleep.

In this first meeting, the baby was sitting in his buggy, gravely staring at me. Father then released him and held him on his knee. As the baby started to grizzle, father made as though to hand him to mother. I said, "What would happen if you kept hold of him?" Father said, "He'll probably start to cry", but he turned Harry towards him and swung him in the air. Harry chuckled, resettled down again on his father's lap. In fact, he stayed there for the rest of the hour of our meeting. It gave us the opportunity to think about how the whole family had begun to believe that only mother could soothe Harry, but that perhaps his father could also do it. When fathers are able to share in the comforting of their baby, it not only lessens the strains on the mother, the father may also gain some authority in stopping the baby from an endless exploitation of the mother. In this method of parent–infant psychotherapy, using the evidence in the room of small examples of behaviour enables the therapist and family to notice and think about their usual way of interacting and the philosophy behind this.

The next time, mother came with Harry on her own because of father's shift work. Father had started to spend more time with the baby. Harry's sleeping had improved a little, and the two parents were actively thinking about how to get him out of their bed and into his cot. Parents first of all need to have their own anxieties acknowledged and also recount their different child-hood histories. Sometimes a great deal of conflicting experience needs to be talked about before parents can be helped in getting together about the sleep problem. I usually find that the baby then quickly responds, and sleeps better.

In this case, it seemed as important to concentrate on mother's sleeping problem as that of her baby. She had told me that after the trauma of her embolism, she had become "pessimistic" about everything. I felt that her use of the word was quite appropriate: it was not the same as being depressed. I commented that by never getting long-enough cycles of sleep, she was missing out on the way that dreaming restores optimism. Hartman (1973) has stated that the ability to maintain an optimistic mood, energy, and self-confidence requires not just sleep itself but, specifically, REM sleep, which comes at the end of each sleep cycle. Similarly, she was missing out on the post-traumatic recuperative process that dreams and nightmares could have provided. Palombo (1978) has talked of the integrating function of dreaming and assimilating experiences into long-term memory. So, ironically, the stresses that led to her lack of sleep were perpetuated by the effects of the sleeplessness.

I believe that sorting out experiences by talking can fulfil some of the missing functions of dreaming. I also suggested that physical exercise, walking, swimming, and so on without the baby could get this mother into the sort of free-associating state where she could lose her watchfulness and thus sleep better and allow her baby also to relax into sleep. This reflective approach was perhaps helpful to a family striving to recover from trauma. When the work finished, the baby was sleeping better.

Conclusion

The value of a child psychotherapist working in the baby clinic of a general practice is two-fold. First is the clinical work of seeing families with infants. Many of the common problems of infancy such as those with sleeping and feeding have an emotional basis. Many families also come openly with relationship and attachment issues. Such families can often be helped within a few meetings. In parent–infant work, we often debate about *who is the patient.* Is it the baby, the parent, or the relationship between them? As I said before, the weighing scales can be thought of as a kind of scales of justice. Relevant to this are some thoughts about justice that I owe to my husband, Eric Rayner (1999), and parent–infant work. Habermas (1990) shows how, in order to achieve fairness, a moment of empathy is essential, leading on to public discussion. He says that justice can only be tested in discussion, and solitary theory is no substitute for this. The moment of empathy is essential: each must put himself or herself into the place of everyone else in discussing whether a proposed norm is fair to all, and this must be done publicly. Arguments played out in the individual consciousness or in the theoretician's mind are no substitute for real discourse. It is interesting to think that the complex attunements of parent–infant psychotherapy are a live example of this real discourse. At best, perhaps therapeutic consultations give families an experience of striving for some degree of justice and fairness to all the parties involved.

Second, this clinical exposure can be put to wider use. Our contact with patients gives us confirmation of theoretical ideas about individual internal processes and family functioning, and particularly about the recognizing and use of feelings stirred up in ourselves by our patients. The real application of the knowledge gained is in sharing it with doctors or health visitors who see many more families than is possible for us.

In CAMHS clinics referrals, even if self-made, have a formal structure, and cases can be "closed". GPs and health visitors, in contrast, have an open-ended relationship with their patients, or clients. As evaluation in all aspects of medical work becomes imperative, a psychotherapist can perhaps back the primary care team in continuing to recognize the importance of the emotional and psychosomatic aspects of their work, and in keeping going over years of dealing with the cumulative experience of seeing patients with undefined needs. On-going consultation with an appreciative outside colleague can help the team both with rigorous standards of keeping to the task and with higher self-appreciation of the value of the work.

CHAPTER THREE

A model for a primary-care-based child and family mental health service

Beverley Tydeman and Patrick Kiernan

We want to describe here a model of work established over the last six years in several GP practices in West London. We explain the context, give a historical overview, and outline the theoretical framework that guides the work as well the nature of referrals, giving some case examples. We provide data on the evaluation of the service, explain how this model provides continuing professional development for the multidisciplinary team in primary care, and consider the future development of the service.

The context

There is an increasing evidence base on the effectiveness of psychoanalytically trained therapists in GP surgeries, although most of the research has been done with therapeutic services offered to adults. Child and adolescent mental health issues are only recently being addressed. It is suggested that about one in ten children has emotional difficulties, with presentation of problems often being with physical symptoms rather than psychological ones. The GP or health visitor may be the professional to whom the child and parent first present. Early intervention in the surgery can prevent later problems and reduce the problem of stigma sometimes associated with mental health services. Some of these difficulties may respond to a few sessions with a well-trained therapist at the surgery.

The wider government agenda for change sets out standards for improvement and modernization of child and adolescent mental health services, stating that psychological well-being and mental health services for children are priorities and are seen as being "everyone's business": primary care, education, social services, youth justice, voluntary organizations, and all who come into contact with children. This requires multi-agency partnership and clinicians who are skilled in cross-boundary work located in the community. Hence local strategies need to reflect the broader push for child-centred services that are easy to access and non-stigmatizing.

At the time that this particular project was conceived, the report *Together We Stand* (Department of Health, 1995) delineated a tiered approach to CAMHS. It acknowledged that psychological disorders in children are very common and that children are less likely to "just grow out of it" than has traditionally been supposed. The document states: "The mental health of children and adolescents is a particularly important area as many are vulnerable to physical, intellectual, emotional, social or behavioural developmental disorders, which if not treated, may have serious implications for their adult life". As Table 3.1 shows, the greatest number of mental health problems are seen in primary care, where very little specialist service is provided.

It is against this background that we established a GP-based child and family therapy service. The pilot project began in 1996 with an outreach psychotherapist from a child and family consultation service offering one half-day a month to a single local general practice. In 1997 funding was withdrawn because of financial cutbacks. However, the health authority stepped in and supported the project so long as clear aims and objectives were agreed. The service was subsequently expanded to two practices. In 1999 one of the authors (PK) put a proposal to the local primary care group (PCG), as it then was, to fund rolling out the service to more GP

TABLE 3.1
**Percentage of children with mental health problems
seen at various tiers of CAMHS services**

Tiers of CAMHS services		Percentage
Tier 1	Primary care/front-line staff	15
Tier 2	Uni-disciplinary specialist, e.g. clinical psychologist	7
Tier 3	Multidisciplinary teams	1.85
Tier 4	Very specialist and inpatient care	0.00075

practices. The PCG had at that time developed a devolved structure of locality groups bringing together natural communities of general practices to take forward locally identified service priorities as well as identify education and training needs. It was decided to site and develop the project across one locality. The project was also in line with PCG priorities, which included adult mental health and child and adolescent mental health. It had a multipractice, multiprofessional approach and aimed to improve clinical standards and maintain continuing education through group case discussion.

The general practice environment offers a unique opportunity for delivering early intervention child and family therapy services. A service sited in primary care was designed to target unmet need, be easily accessible, non-stigmatizing, cost-effective, coordinated, and efficient. It was designed to operationalize Tier 1 of the CAMHS approach in order to form part of the care pathway and produce collaborative working with other mental health services.

The service

The service is currently provided by multidisciplinary teams consisting of fifteen GPs working across five practices, three practice attached health visitors, practice nurses, and two psychotherapists. The two psychotherapists involved are psychoanalytically trained, one in adult psychotherapy and the other in child psychotherapy, with both having extensive experience of working in CAMHS and a detailed knowledge of the local professional network and local services for children and adolescents. The number of children aged 0–18 years registered across the project is 4,900, representing 15% of the registered population of 32,267. Currently five practices receive five to six hours of therapist time each per month, at fortnightly sessions. Where possible, the service runs alongside and is integral to the baby clinics in each practice. The service offers both short-term, focused family psychotherapy within the practice setting and initial assessment and referral on to other services within CAMHS, or to other appropriate services.

The service offers a model of working where therapeutic contracts are established within the context of shared working with other members of the primary care team. Support is given to health visitors who have strategically important roles in prevention and early intervention. The psychotherapists offer brief interventions to unblock some obstacles to a child's developmental progress in ordinary family life. Where there is more complex and deep-rooted pathology, the child is fast-tracked straight to Tier 3 services. What we hope to provide is effective treatment that is an accurate therapeutic "dose"—not too long and not too short: the least help needed to release a child from an impasse and to get families back on track.

All children and adolescents (age 0–18) who are registered at the five practices in the locality and suitable for brief intervention are eligible for referral to the service. Referrals are made to the therapist by the GP, the health visitor, or the practice nurse. Such referrals may take place at the time of the baby clinic or from any routine clinic session. A first appointment is offered to the child/family as soon as possible. Up to eight appointments are offered per patient/family within the practice setting. Feedback is provided to the referring GPs and health visitors within the practice team. Confidentiality is shared by the team. Sometimes families return after the first "dose" of treatment, needing some more input, perhaps for a different family member, or later in the development of the originally referred child. This we have come to call a "revolving door" policy.

The following are some of the reasons for referral to the primary-care-based service for each of age groups. A brief case vignette from each developmental stage, written by the therapist concerned (BT) will illustrate some aspects of our work.

Infants, preschool children, and their parents

Reasons for referral in this age group include:

- difficulties with feeding or weaning;
- sleeping problems;
- difficulties with separating, including crying and clinging;
- toilet-training problems;
- sibling rivalry;
- oppositional behaviour manifested by the child.

Mothers with postnatal depression are seen with their infants or on their own if they need a space away from their baby for the moment. However, we are alert to the issue of mothers not wishing to be burdened with diagnoses that some feel are set in concrete and their feelings of being overwhelmed and depleted are understood in terms of their current situation, which is temporary. Attachment issues come up regularly, as do issues relating to father's role in child-rearing. Most of the cases referred fall within these categories. In order to protect confidentiality, all clinical examples are fictionalized, but based on compilations of real situations.

Case study: "Julie" and her baby, "Ella"

A GP referred Julie because she was becoming increasingly anxious about her 11-month-old baby's health and development, thinking that "there must be something wrong with her because she's so clingy, unsettled, she cries all the time and is difficult to soothe". Julie was visiting the surgery frequently and had asked for antidepressants as she was finding it hard to cope and was not getting enough sleep. In the first meeting with this young mother, she poured out her troubles while her baby,

Ella, slept in the buggy in the room. I learned that she and her partner were getting extremely irritable with each other. This baby had not been planned, but after some thought they both felt it was a "happy accident" and were delighted when she was born. They had not realized what an impact a baby would have on their lives, with the father being particularly upset about the loss of spontaneity in their lives now, as opposed to when they had just been a couple and had enjoyed a very busy social life. Julie felt unsupported and criticized in her role as a mother, as her partner was often away on business and he worked long hours. She was thinking that they were starting to drift apart. She spoke of missing her own family, who lived abroad. She had a network of friends but missed her job and her colleagues and the structure to the day that work had provided. She had given up her job, as she wanted to give her full attention to Ella, feeling that she had been deprived of her own mother when she was an infant, because her mother had had a successful career. She wanted to give her baby what she herself had not had. Now she was unhappy and sometimes wished she didn't have a baby.

When Ella woke up towards the end of the session, after taking her out of the buggy, Julie did not hold her close to her body but at arms' length, facing outwards, so that there could be no eye contact. Ella's eyes searched around, latching on to mine. Without going in to all the details, the work consisted of containing Julie's anxieties about Ella's state, through thinking with her about how Ella's moods may be closely connected to her own emotional state. When she felt she was listened to and understood, she could do the same for her baby. She came to value herself as a mother more fully, and although her partner was never able to come to any of the sessions, she began to think of him in a more benign way, appreciating that he did contribute to family life when he could. By the third session she was considering weaning Ella in a gradual way, and we spoke about how painful it would be for Ella to give up something she has enjoyed so much. It would be a loss for both of them. She was now much more connected to Ella, feeling for her as a separate person, with a mind and feelings of her own. There was much more eye contact and moments of pleasurable "peekaboo" play together on the floor of the consulting-room. By the fifth session it was clear that this mother and infant pair were back on track.

Schoolchildren

Reasons for referral include:

- conduct disorders, including hyperactivity or attention deficit;
- psychosomatic problems;
- anxiety and unhappiness;
- aggression, antisocial behaviour, peer difficulties, school refusal, and bullying.

Case study: "Hanan" and her son, "Ibrahim"

A health visitor was concerned about an asylum-seeker who had fled her country of origin and had arrived in London four months prior to referral. She was in an extremely agitated state about her younger son, who was finding it difficult to sleep and waking up with nightmares. When I (BT) first met this mother with her 2-year-old son, Ibrahim, and his 6-year-old brother, we organized an Arabic interpreter. Hanan spoke about how terrible her life was—she had not had any contact with her husband since leaving the Sudan and did not know whether he was alive or dead. Both of them had been interrogated by government forces, and her husband had been imprisoned. The husband managed to arrange for the family, which also included two teenage daughters, to get away and come to England.

In the first meeting we focused on the concerns she had about her older son. He was shy and had deep rings under his large, sad eyes. She said his nightmare was about robbers coming into their room to take their things away and threatening to kill them. He cried and could not stop crying. In the morning he did not want to go to his new school and complained of tummy-ache. Depending on how robust she felt, she was able to get him to school on some occasions, but on others she felt unable to do anything. When she felt incapacitated, she let many of her maternal duties fall on her older daughters, who came in for later sessions.

The work with this family was very painful, filled as it was with anguish, loss, and terror; it was not post-traumatic stress that was the issue so much as continuing, ongoing trauma about finding a safe place for the family. The pains in the tummy were spoken about in emotional terms, linked to the loss and worry about Ibrahim's father, the family's exposure to civil war, and their home and country being taken away from them. This was also connected to the content of the nightmares and the extreme fear about whether life can go on.

What is most striking about working with such cases in primary care is the extent of the anxiety conveyed. This can be so great that ordinary "maternal preoccupation" breaks down. When the parents' mental state is disturbed, the safety of the children is at stake. These families use the medical practice as a kind of safe haven where they are listened to, and the families often have a lot of appointments with many services. When there are many family members, more workers often need to be brought in.

Both mother and Ibrahim were able to convey a potential for thoughtfulness and resilience. His symptoms subsided, but mother's state deteriorated as she began to feel more and more powerless. It became important to communicate with other members of the professional network, particularly the community psychiatric nurse involved in mother's care. As with many of these families, the solicitor asked for psychological reports in support of the family's asylum application. A solid emotional contact developed with this family, whose members began to flourish. It was a terrible shock to all the professionals involved when they were suddenly relocated without the opportunity to have a final meeting.

Adolescents

Reasons for referral include:

- identity issues;
- relationships with parents and peers;
- depression;
- substance misuse;
- eating disorders;
- antisocial activities or underachievement;
- self-harm;
- disability.

Case Study: "Marie"

A GP was concerned about this beautiful and very clever 14-year-old girl whose mother had brought her in to be weighed and assessed as to whether she was developing an eating disorder. For the past six months Marie had not menstruated. In every other way she was a perfect child who had never been a problem. She was the first-born in a large family. Most of the eight sessions were with mother and Marie, but I managed to get father in for one session as well. This was because it seemed vital to have his particular contribution and point of view. After two assessment sessions, during which time the therapist was in contact with the GP who was doing the weekly weighing, together they decided that a referral to the hospital was necessary. Marie was failing to gain weight, and this generated sufficient anxiety to want the involvement of the hospital in case she needed to be admitted as an inpatient.

The Tier 3 service at the hospital was able to respond rapidly, and outpatient appointments were offered, while continuing with sessions at the GP practice. During these sessions it emerged that Marie had felt repudiated by her father, whom she had seen by chance in close physical proximity to another man. He had denied this, but later, after a session with Marie and her father, during which I broached this incident, he admitted it had happened, and he was sorry to have caused any hurt. Mother and father managed to start addressing some of the issues brought up by the incident. Marie began to put on weight and avoided having to go in to hospital. In the first session after the break she told me she wanted to have much bigger breasts, and she hoped she would put weight on in the right places. The brief family work had managed to help them get back on track, and Marie could accept her developing sexuality and femininity, possibly linked to the more honest relationship between her parents. The success of this was probably largely due to the close working relationship between the therapist and the GP within the surgery, as well as the input from the hospital department. Marie's physical care was kept in mind, while some understanding was gained about the emotional elements of the family situation and the gender and sexuality issues involved.

Sometimes it will not be appropriate to begin an intervention, and the therapist will advise the referrer to refer directly to Tier 3 and 4 services. This is usually the case where there are complex intergenerational issues or where families have had long-standing contact with mental health or social services. At other times an assessment will be done in the GP practice, and the therapist is aware that a multidisciplinary team and longer-term intervention is required. She will then refer on to the appropriate service.

The theoretical framework that guides our work

Short-term and focused family psychotherapy is a way of working with families that enables them to draw on their own strengths and resources in order to move towards a more effective way of resolving interpersonal problems. This concurs with a wider general practice counselling strategy that aims to support shorter, more focused interventions in the primary care setting. Where appropriate, all family members are offered a service directly or indirectly by way of the family appointments. These sessions work explicitly with the patterns of relationships and communication within the family group, while being based on a solid knowledge of children's psychological development.

Therapeutic work in primary care requires a flexibility of approach and an ability to think quickly. A space for thinking is offered to try to understand a child's behaviour. We aim to come to a sensitive understanding of the unconscious processes involved, as well as comprehension of the broader systemic networks. While it is most usual for an individual child to be presented as the identified patient, there is almost always more than one patient in the room—for example, very worried parents—as well as the obviously symptomatic child. We try to think about the meaning of the child's behaviour in the context of the family situation. We use observational skills and pay very careful attention to what is going on in the "here and now" in front of our eyes. As well as observing what is going on "out there", we also pay particular attention to the feelings aroused inside ourselves while in the presence of these family members.

There is a powerful force field of emotional currents in family life that we feel it is important to address. Most families come at a time of heightened emotional arousal, feeling at the end of their tether and at a loss. Reassuring predictability has gone, and they want some help. They usually want confusion to be rendered meaningful, coherence to return, and effective action to be prescribed. In such states, most people find it hard to think for themselves, and they need some thinking to be done on their behalf. Listening to the outpouring of high levels of distress cannot be regarded as "just" listening. In such consultations the clinician is working hard by "taking in" and experiencing painful emotions and thinking about them, rather than being overwhelmed by them. A parallel process happens with mothers and their babies. To some people this process might not be considered "work", but for psychotherapists it is a crucial part of our job that we call "containment".

The psychoanalyst Wilfred Bion (1962) coined the concept "container–contained", which he based on the ordinary way a mother makes life bearable for her baby. She takes in the distress related to hunger, pain, wind, cold, fear of falling—a muddle of bad experiences—into her own mind and processes them herself in order to soothe the distressed baby. According to Bion, this, in turn, sets in motion the thinking process in the baby's mind. As a consequence of being thought about, the baby can feel recognized, known, and understood and can develop a thinking apparatus of his own. The mother can do this better for her baby if she has developed a reflective space inside herself, related to her own experience of having another person's containing presence available to her. By being thought about and understood, she can regain her own thinking capacity. Being this containing person is hard work and requires one to restrain the urge to act prematurely to put an end to the mental pain the patient is projecting into us. Sometimes we do not know the answer, and we are unable to resolve the uncertainty instantly. We hope to offer a "good-enough" consultation or series of sessions.

Evaluation of the service

Since it was established, we have collected data on the service for evaluation purposes. In this section we report on this data.

Service activity

In 2002, 84 children (individually or with other family members) were referred to the service; 202 appointments were available. The five participating practices started to use the service at different points during the year, so uptake of the appointments varied. Figure 3.1 shows the percentage of available appointments during 2002 that were attended, not attended, or cancelled. Attendance rates are high compared to secondary care. With the information now available, we are able to set quality standards around issues such as waiting times for appointments and rates of non-attendance. It also has to be acknowledged that there are opportunities for further research in this area of work.

Clients seen

The majority of referrals to the service during 2002 were for children under five, reflecting the close working of the service with

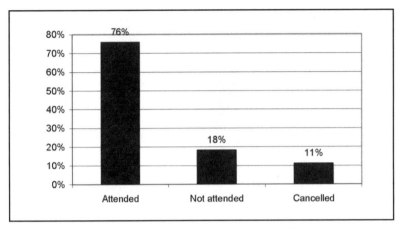

FIGURE 3.1   Appointments for child and family therapy services

the baby clinics, which more easily encompasses emotional as well as physical health within its remit. There was an increase during the year of referrals for children aged 6–12 and adolescents. The majority of families were white, but about one third were from black and ethnic minority groups, including many refugee families from Kosovo and the Middle East (included under "other"). A profile of the people using the service during 2002 is shown by age (Figure 3.2), gender (Figure 3.3), and ethnicity (Figure 3.4).

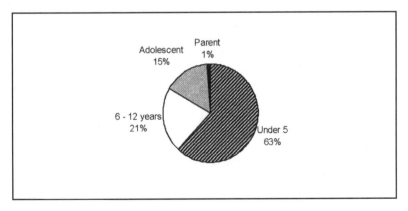

FIGURE 3.2   Age range of presenting client

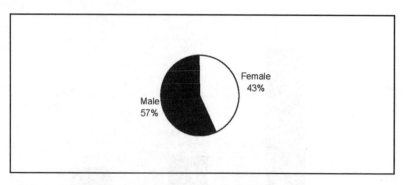

FIGURE 3.3   Gender of children seen

Problems identified and addressed in therapy

As Figure 3.5 shows, family relationships dominated the list of problems seen in 2002. This supports the need for a family- as well as a child-orientated service. The wide range of other problems is also indicated.

Outcome

During 2002 we also asked therapists to collate data on whether they regarded work as completed and how successful they judged the outcome to be. The survey was of all cases seen that year. In Figure 3.6, "complete" means that the therapist and patient or patients have agreed a shared ending. Those who "withdrew" did so without discussion but not necessarily without improvement. "Referral on" means those patients who were referred to more specialist child and adolescent mental health services or to more specific services within the community, such as the marriage guidance service or the child development centre. In addition, there was a considerable number of "ongoing" cases where the outcome was as yet unknown but perhaps reflected the containment of the problems within the primary care setting.

Figure 3.7 shows the therapist's clinical assessment at discharge.

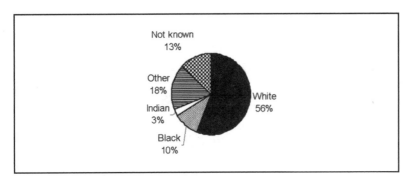

FIGURE 3.4   Ethnicity of children seen

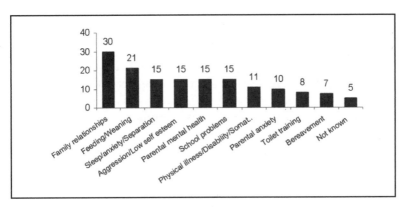

FIGURE 3.5   Problem category

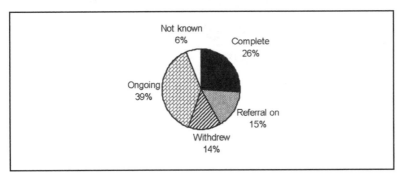

FIGURE 3.6   Outcome of child and family therapy

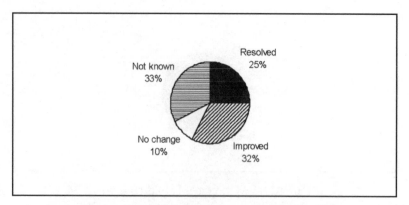

FIGURE 3.7   Clinical assessment at discharge

Patient satisfaction

During 2002 we also carried out a patient satisfaction survey. This shows high levels of satisfaction in general (Figure 3.8), as well as with the ease of making appointments (Figure 3.9) and, most especially, with the siting of the appointments (Figure 3.10). Perhaps most significantly, Figure 3.11 illustrates the largely positive perceptions that families had of the overall benefits of the service.

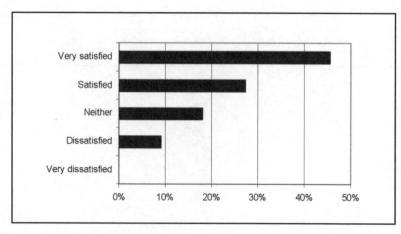

FIGURE 3.8   Overall satisfaction with the service

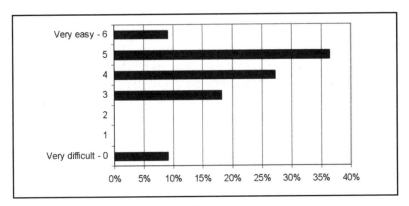

FIGURE 3.9   Ease of getting an appointment

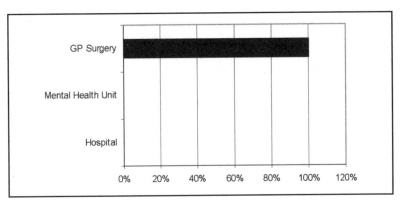

FIGURE 3.10   Where would you prefer to be seen?

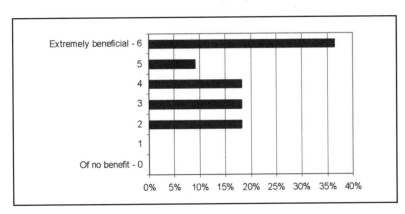

FIGURE 3.11   Overall benefit from the service

53

Education and continuing professional development

Continuing education and training of all those involved in providing the service is integral to the project, and its foundation is based in multi-practice, multidisciplinary, reflective learning. It also serves as a supporting structure for the team. All practices involved meet every two months for clinical discussions and exchange of ideas relating to child and family mental health issues. These meetings cover business matters but are primarily focused on clinical presentations.

Through group interaction, the psychotherapists, GPs, health visitors, and practice nurses learn more about each other's frames of reference. We exchange ideas and think together about emotional reactions to patients, such as why people can become dependent, reject help, be over-involved with their children, have self-defeating attitudes, and the many "odd" ways people have of living their lives. Invariably after lively discussion we come away from these reflections feeling supported and having more energy, competence, curiosity, enthusiasm, and respect for human foibles. Thinking about our own shortcomings helps us better tolerate the vulnerability of others. While these discussions often tap into an internal space, there is also an academic side to them that helps us feel sustained by mutual learning.

Organizational issues include subjects such as the number of sessions to be offered without blocking access for new referrals; how soon a patient who has completed the allocated sessions may return for further work ("revolving door"); the process of referral on to CAMHS or, if appropriate, adult mental health services. The project also explores developmental issues such as its role in antenatal care, community outreach work, and linking with local schools.

Future developments

The service has developed over the years from one general practice to all practices in a locality grouping. We are keen to expand across the whole of the primary care trust (PCT) and include:

- offering the service as a model for practices to other localities in the PCT and across other PCTs;
- regularly reviewing the project through the ongoing monitoring mechanisms;
- commissioning further research as well as continuing the education and training components;
- establishing a PCT/national norm for service delivery.

With increased demand and the uncovering of unmet need, it would be necessary to have at least six hours per month of psychotherapists' time per thousand registered patients aged 0–18 years. This may be adjusted locally to take into account varying population needs. We also hope to establish and develop links with wider community services such as social services, as well as through schools and nurseries through mental health link workers.

CHAPTER FOUR

A systemic outreach clinic in primary care: which tier is that?

Rob Senior and Robert Mayer

The family clinic at the Highgate Group Practice was established some fifteen years ago and has been described else where (Graham, Senior, Lazarus, Mayer, & Asen, 1992; Senior, 1994). In its current form, the clinic has no formal link with the Tavistock Clinic, but one of the authors (RS), who now works at the Tavistock, was a member of the original team and continues to provide infrequent consultation and supervision to the team. This chapter locates the clinic within the wider culture of general practice and mental health services. We bring the story of the clinic up to date and describe, with illustrations, the more recent work of the team as it has extended into the local community.

We have described previously the way in which the context of the clinic not only permitted its development but also shaped the style and nature of the clinical work. By "context" we mean the relationships within the practice between professionals and with patients as well as the wider political influences on the commissioning and delivery of health services. It is our belief that the recursive influences of the context on the practice and vice versa continue to be important. If models of intervention do not fit the context or lack sufficient flexibility, they are unlikely to succeed. With this in mind, we also consider the place of an initiative like the family clinic within the rapidly changing map of general practice and ask more specifically what role such a clinic may have in a comprehensive child and family mental health service.

The early years

The project was first established in May 1989. Its aim was to provide a family therapy clinic within the context of a large group family practice in north London. One of the GPs and the practice social worker had considerable family therapy experience. A family therapist who was engaged at the time in advanced training in family therapy was also invited in order to form a small team. Later, a GP trainee and another GP from the practice joined. The clinic arose from the interest and commitment of some members of the practice, and some very important changes had already taken place in the thinking of the practice, which made the setting up of the clinic possible. It was a model that evolved from within the practice.

What were the influences on this process? In this practice, the lunchtime primary health care meeting (a multidisciplinary meeting where cases are discussed) had a long history as a thinking space. Over time, the model that informed the meeting had evolved from one that was psychodynamically based and that paid attention to group processes to a more "systemically" orientated one. The original model had first developed from a pioneering social work attachment from the Tavistock Clinic in the 1970s (Graham & Sher, 1976) and had served the practice well in helping the professionals understand the conflicts that are sometimes enacted within the health care team, and the professionals' own feelings that can be aroused. However, the "fit" between this way of thinking and the nature of general practice had changed. Psychodynamically oriented Balint groups had become less influential. The paternalism of medical practice was being challenged, and within the doctor–patient relationship the doctor could increasingly be seen as the person who was "stuck". The interest in systemic ideas gave a different and frequently more creative flavour to the team meetings and allowed for better networking between patients, their families, and the professionals involved (McDaniel, Hepworth, & Doherty, 1992).

The kind of "thinking space" described above may be taken for granted by professionals working in mental health settings, but for GPs who are used to ten-minute consultations it can be seen as a luxury rather than an essential part of the work. Of course, "thinking" in the practice has always taken place in many other contexts that are often unconnected. Outside the consultation itself, there is "gossip" or casual conversation between GP partners or with practice nurse, health visitor, or counsellor, all of which can provide feedback to a practitioner or shed light on a question, doubt, or dilemma. The more formal meeting provides a space for these information streams to be connected, examined, and reflected back. For example, a GP may find that an anxiety presented by a parent is mirrored or confirmed, or alternatively may be reassured by learning, for example, about a health visitor's contact with the children. A picture can emerge informed by multiple perspectives and new possibilities for all the participants. Of course, in other settings these practice clinical meetings can take many forms, including consultations with visiting specialists who may be conducting shifted out-patients. However, in the Highgate Practice the change in the style of the meeting paved the way for the setting up of the family clinic by introducing a different way of conceptualizing problems.

Once the family clinic had been established, attendance became one of a number of possible outcomes emerging from these formal and informal conversations. However, it has never been the most usual outcome, the clinic representing an atypical and relatively expensive concentration of thinking for a primary care context. More often, discussions at the meeting allow the practitioners to continue their work feeling more enabled, possibly to invite a colleague to join in a consultation or visit, or to allow them to acknowledge that a resource outside the practice is required and appropriate, rather than to soldier on unsupported. The form and nature of the practice clinical meetings thus prefigured and facilitated the development of the clinic. The presence of the clinic, in turn, continues to influence the meeting not only by being a reassuring internal resource but also by directly informing the thinking of the meeting.

What is the clinic like?

The clinic takes place on one half-day a fortnight, the venue being a large practice common-room that is usefully different from the "surgery" and has the benefit of a video link to an observing-room. Historically, most referrals have come from the other clinical members of the practice—usually GPs or practice nurses, but also the practice counsellor and health visitors. They are written but often arise from the multidisciplinary practice meetings described above where troubled families are discussed. Responses to referral include, but are not limited to, a formal appointment for the family. For those readers with an interest in systemic ideas and practice, the clinic has been greatly influenced by the "post-Milan" thinking of Cecchin and others (Cecchin, 1987) and makes extensive use of the reflecting team and other "in-the-room" collaborative ideas (Andersen, 1987). Writing and thinking about narrative approaches has recently also created a very useful bridge between primary care and systemic therapy (Greenhalgh & Hurwitz, 1998; Launer, 2002; White & Epston, 1990).

The personnel of the clinic has grown slowly over the years, and there are currently five members: three GPs, a counsellor with family therapy, mediation, and social work training, and an external therapist, funded initially by the health authority and now by the primary care trust. In addition, there is usually a student on placement for a year from one of the family therapy training centres. The clinic also provides a continuing base for teaching medical students and GP registrars (Mayer & Graham, 1998). Although the majority of family problems have concerned children and young people, this is not always the case. The oldest client approached the practice when he was 96 (Louden & Graham, 1998)!

The clinic has continued to invite referrals from across the age range within the practice. Between a quarter and a third of referrals from clinicians in the practice involve adults and couples, including some patients with identified adult mental health difficulties.

However, rightly or wrongly, the outside world has tended to identify the clinic (and family therapy provision generally) as belonging within a child and adolescent mental health service (CAMHS). Throughout much of the existence of the clinic, the local CAMHS service has also experienced major difficulties with long waiting lists and a restricted range of services. As discussed below, this has had the effect of making local commissioners interested in the clinic as an alternative way of delivering CAMHS services rather than as a more general mental health service.

Some recent developments

From the outset, the perception that the clinic provided a valuable service to the patients and partners in the practice helped to ensure its establishment and survival, but there have, of course, been other forces at work. Despite the recognition gained over a number of years, including an NHS "Beacon" award, the clinic has struggled at times to achieve adequate or reliable funding. A number of beliefs have prevailed in the funding authority at various times. One commissioner of services argued that the clinic need not be funded separately from the rest of the practice because of a belief that the overall workload would fall as a result of reduced consultation rates. It was even suggested that the drugs bill for tranquillizers and antidepressants would drop as a consequence of successful therapy. The team were sufficiently interested in the first hypothesis to look and see what happened to consultation rates following referral to the clinic. It was indeed true that, for some families, referral marked the end of a period of multiple consultations by different members. Equally, however, there were families who had hardly been in the surgery, where referral appeared to be the appropriate beginning of a number of consultations, including individual appointments with their GP; a teenager with an eating disorder was a graphic example of just such a predicament.

Eventually, the success of the clinic in persuading the local budget-holders that the work deserved to be funded led to a problem at a different level: the problem of equity.

In terms of the local health care community this meant that the practice's own patients could not be seen to have a service if the other patients within the same primary care trust did not have access as well. As a result, the PCT indicated that the team could still only be paid for the work if it was made more widely available. It was clear that the team could never hope to offer the same practice-based service to another 40 practices without being immediately overwhelmed, especially at a time when the local CAMHS had virtually ground to a halt. They decided to ask the neighbouring practices what they would like from a service. The results of this survey indicated that, although the ability to refer cases traditionally was valued, there was also interest in telephone consultation, joint meetings with the referrer, and consultations at the outreach surgery.

The members of the clinic team experienced a great deal of scepticism about the value of expansion. After all, the presumed strength of the original model was dependent on local knowledge and the possibility of easy conversations within the practice team. There was a risk that the clinic might be no more helpful to other practices than traditional secondary referrals to which they already had access. Indeed, it seemed as if the success of the clinic had, paradoxically, led to an invitation to take on a more conventional "specialist" role and recreate the very problems the original clinic had been established to solve. In line with other specialist services that want to be helpful but need to protect scarce resources, the team therefore envisaged providing principally consultation/liaison to outside referrers, with little in the way of direct work with families. Alternatively, joint meetings that included the referrer and the family might generate new ideas to help the referrer to continue to work with the family. A helpful telephone call might make a referral unnecessary by supporting the practitioner or indicating where specialist referral was clearly indicated.

In fact, all these options have now been tried with different families, alongside more traditional appointments in either the Highgate Practice or the referring practice. Certainly, feedback from families and practices so far indicates that for some the opportunity of being seen in their own practice is highly valued, but some were more than happy to travel to another local practice. Access to transport clearly plays a part here.

Within the practice itself there has always been a variation in the rate of referrals to the family clinic, but in general lulls are short-lived and followed by periods of considerable activity. This has also been mirrored in the pattern of outreach referrals. At the point when we have started to think that we should be reminding GPs about what is on offer, the need to do this is then obviated by an influx of new referrals. Currently we have a steady flow of work, which we are able to incorporate into our regular clinic day by meeting at an earlier time. Because we have several therapists, we are able to double up and see two extra families, whether in our own practice or elsewhere (mainly at the patients' practice).

Efficient administration is essential to ensure optimal use of time. We allocate a mid-point time to deal with both practical issues and professional practice. On a really intense day we may not have as much time as we would want for preparation and debriefing, but we do recognize the importance of having adequate time for reflecting on our work, and systems for peer and external supervision are built in. Gradually we have become more flexible at filling appointments that are cancelled at short notice (often—but not always—for valid reasons). When patients fail to show up without warning, we generally respond with a quick telephone call to establish the cause. Tightening up our practice has paid dividends, and in the main we are very fully occupied. Unfortunately this leaves little time for valuable activities such as research.

Referrals are discussed at the family clinic, and we aim to respond within a week by telephoning the referrer. Two therapists work together with a family, and the lead therapist will then contact the family by telephone to arrange an initial meeting. Usually we see families in their own doctor's surgery. We always invite the referrer to be present at the initial meeting, but this has often been declined. Where our offer has been taken up, the response of the GPs and practice nurses has been extremely positive. They report that they have found it useful in acquiring new ideas and approaches that they can use in further contact with the family and, indeed, with other families.

Our approach is, above all, to be flexible. On one occasion when the patient did not attend the appointment, the time was spent consulting with the practice nurse. On another occasion, when the patient did not attend at her GP's surgery, we noticed that the appointment time had been mistyped and paid an impromptu home visit. Our effort to ensure that the opportunity to meet was not lost was rewarded with an extremely productive session. Our general impression is that GPs are often using the service for families where the GP finds it difficult to access help elsewhere, because of long waits, poor fit between the problem and the available service, or reluctance on the part of families to engage with a more formal mental health service. This is in contrast to our work in the family clinic, where we are usually the first port of call. The nature of the work can therefore be different, and there may be barriers to overcome in terms of patient expectations of failure. The kinds of referrals in this category most often include separated parents in conflict over contact with children, adolescents in trouble, and school refusal. As a consequence of these and other factors, including funding, the outreach work more closely resembles the remit of a traditional CAMHS than our own in-house referrals, which have developed over time in response to developments in the GP's own systemic skills and interests, as well as our broadening definition of what constitutes an "appropriate" referral.

On the whole, this way of working has been of most interest to practice nurses, counsellors, and GPs in training rather than to established GPs. This may tell us something about the time pressures GPs are under—or perhaps that we have not explained ourselves well enough. Either way, we have ended up doing a substantial amount of direct work with families. In many ways the referrals are no different from those we are used to receiving internally, except that they are more child- and adolescent-focused since this is how we have advertised ourselves, and are drawn from a population that is more ethnically diverse than our own. We need to develop our competencies working where English is not a first language or is not spoken at all. Generally we go out to practices in pairs. Sometimes families come to our practice, or we go to their homes. Our feedback so far from families and referrers suggests that the service is valued, and we are considering how to make it more widely available without compromising our ability to function as a team.

Illustrations of the work

The following two cases are invented but comprise elements from a number of cases to illustrate the kind of work done by the outreach team.

Case study: "Mahmoud" and his family

The team was asked by a GP from a local practice to see a teenage boy, Mahmoud, who was worrying his mother by his behaviour and who had recently been in trouble with the police over a violent incident for which he was going to be charged. Mother, Zehara, is from Morocco. In addition to Mahmoud, there is a younger daughter, Saffa, aged 8. There is a history in the referral of past maternal alcoholism. Mahmoud was thought possibly to have foetal alcohol syndrome and was born with some facial abnormalities. The children's father had left the family shortly after Saffa was born and was not in contact. After discussion with the referrer, we decided to see the family in the context of the GP's surgery, where we knew mother felt safe.

We discovered that Zehara was very appreciative of her GP, even deciding not to move in order to remain in the area. However, she felt very criticized and disempowered in relation to mental health professionals and social services. Indeed, she felt betrayed by a counsellor who, she believed, had made a blaming report about her, suggesting that she might be unfit to be a mother, although social services did not find evidence to place the children on the child protection register. Zehara was an apparently likeable and concerned mother who, with the help of a supportive partner—a doctor considerably older than herself—had rescued herself from her alcoholism and was devoting her life to providing the best for her children. The doctor had acted as a father to Mahmoud particularly, but, sadly, he had died relatively recently. Mahmoud was clearly grieving his loss.

We have now met six times. In our early sessions, we felt that the family had been helped by establishing a contract between mother and son whereby they attempted reciprocally to achieve some simple, mutually agreed goals. It became clear that Zehara very much valued coming to the sessions, even though the problems with her son had not been completely resolved. We hypothesized that she was responding to being valued and respected. We were a little apprehensive about our role as a systemic family team, particularly in the light of Zehara's assertions that she could never trust another counsellor and get help for herself in that way and that she would like to meet and talk regularly.

We reflected that we have met only six times in a year and a half, and that she and her son are managing their difficulties during his passage through adolescence. Seeing Zehara without her son in one recent session, we have begun to understand how culturally shaming it is for her to admit to her family in Morocco and to Mahmoud himself that he has no substantive father figure. We offered an additional perspective: that Mahmoud, although loyal to many of his mother's cultural beliefs, might value, as a father, the man who had looked after him and loved him until his recent death. We explored openly with Zehara whether the family session can be a safe place for her to tell what she calls "the truth" about Mahmoud's real father, which she feels he is ready to know but she finds it impossibly difficult to talk about at home.

We could be said to be adopting a general practice perspective in this case—seeing it as appropriate to continue to be involved regularly but infrequently while Mahmoud is moving towards manhood. We think that the use of a general practice surgery as a meeting place is important. It is interesting that over quite a number of months Zehara has not needed to consult her GP.

Zehara was seen for one more meeting. She described Mahmoud as behaving better and feeling happier. He has asked his mother not to go into details about his father at the moment and reassured her that he will ask when he wants to know more. We have agreed not to arrange another meeting and are leaving them to contact us if they want more help. We will contact them in six months to "keep in touch".

Case study: "Sarah" and her family

Another local GP referred Sarah. She was 17, in the sixth form at school, and seemed to be developing an eating disorder. Her mother had expressed increasing worry about her daughter's idiosyncratic eating and weight loss over a period of a few months, but attempts to talk about the worry had failed, and relationships were increasingly strained. Sarah's father, a successful journalist, felt excluded and was more or less instructed not to intrude on the desperate battles that Sarah and her mother were engaged in. Her younger brother, 13, was sullen and overweight and spent long hours on his Playstation. Sarah had always been a little anxious and obsessional. For a while after her maternal grandmother died when she was 11, she was scared to go in lifts and missed some time from school, but this now seemed behind her; and she had recently done well in her AS levels and was hoping to go to university the following year.

The referring GP mentioned that while he had seen both Sarah and her mother individually, it had not proved possible to get them in the same room. Their accounts were quite different. Although it was clear that Sarah was worryingly thin, he felt she was willing to tackle her eating and had suggested a referral to the practice counsellor, which she was considering. Her mother wanted her to see a specialist but felt that at 17 this could not be forced upon her. The GP felt burdened by the impasse and the worrying prospect of Sarah's health deteriorating further, which was confirmed by her further weight loss of nearly one kilogram a week.

The family clinic considered the referral as one where, although specialist intervention was likely to prove necessary, we might nonetheless serve a useful role in early engagement and facilitation in the process of engagement and escalation within the care pathway.

Following Lock (2002) and the Maudsley approach, we offered at short notice an emergency meeting in the practice, which included the referring GP. He agreed to telephone the family members and insist that they—at least parents and Sarah—attend, which they did. At the meeting, which was serious in tone, the therapist, with the help of the team, was able to elicit a more agreed description of the situation. Father's previously unheard worries were echoed by that of Sarah's GP, who described the anxiety of retaining medical responsibility of her increasingly unstable care. Both Sarah and her mother were able to listen to the worries expressed without experiencing criticism and in a way that seemed to allow the possibility of "uniting against anorexia" rather than battling each other. The meeting had a powerful impact on all attendees and ended with an agreement to arrange an emergency referral to the adolescent eating disorders service, which subsequently ensued.

Although the family clinic is not the provider of "treatment" that is seen as the province of a specialist service, it was able to play a useful role in allowing an intervention that might otherwise have been dangerously delayed. Involving the referrer as part of the system seemed to us an important factor.

The primary care context

The time when the clinic was established was one of considerable optimism in primary care. The political language of the time referred to a "primary-care-led NHS". Fund-holding and locality commissioning, although designed to curtail hospital spending, seemed to offer real power to GPs and others in the primary care team to determine priorities. Creative use was being made of money for health promotion and GP education. The unique, pluralist nature of general practice and its "cradle-to-grave" commitment to health care seemed to be finding a political voice with the establishment of Primary Care Groups (the forerunners of the PCTs). In this climate of optimism, one of the authors (RS) was involved with a number of other practices in setting up versions of the family clinic. Mental health and psychological well-being were clearly on the primary care map. This optimism was carried over briefly into the New Labour government but was replaced fairly rapidly by the now familiar "command and control" ethic, with targets designed to reduce waiting lists and deliver the National Service Frameworks (NSFs). PCTs would now be evaluated and given star ratings according to their perceived ability to deliver on these targets.

This centrally driven public health agenda has many highly desirable aims but has, inadvertently, threatened to change the nature of primary care. Not only has the climate been less propitious for setting up initiatives not considered to be "priorities", but with new access arrangements and appointment targets, the personal and family nature of general practice has been strongly challenged. Mental health is striking for the low priority it is given in the new contract for GPs, which has also failed to anticipate the emerging developments in child and adolescent mental health. Unlike other special interests, there are currently no incentives to encourage GPs to grasp this particular nettle. Despite an acknowledgement that many consultations are about mental health, the majority of mental health problems are managed exclusively in primary care, and the "whole family" opportunities presented are unique. The purpose of describing these shifting contexts is not in order to promote a particular ideology, but to illustrate how the wider context can facilitate or constrain new developments. After all, at the time of writing a new chapter in this story is about to be written with a retreat from central control and a return to "localism", with practice-based commissioning and the encouragement of unique local arrangements. All of this, allied to patient choice and the money that follows, may recreate the conditions for innovation around child and family mental health in primary care.

The CAMHS Context

It is only relatively recently that child and adolescent mental health has become well established as an area in need of prioritized additional funding. Indeed, another considerable influence on the establishment of the clinic was the crisis in resources in the local CAMHS clinics. Since then, real increases in funding have come to local authorities and more recently to PCTs to deliver an expanded CAMHS. Alongside this, interest in primary health care as a context for the delivery of CAMHS has waxed and waned over the last few years. The Health Advisory Service thematic review, *Together*

We Stand (Department of Health, 1995), introduced the idea of a four-tier service in which primary health care was part of "Tier 1", alongside other professionals with direct contact with children but without specialist training. It was innovative at the time because it acknowledged the importance of primary health care in the delivery of mental health interventions for children and families and proposed support, supervision, and training for Tier 1 staff to come from more specialist services. More recently, the National Service Framework for Children (Department of Health, 2004) has also recommended the provision of community-based services, within which primary health care is one context, alongside others such as schools, Sure Start schemes, and children's centres. Indeed, primary care is explicitly used in the NSF document to refer to all front-line services that have contact with children and their families. The centre of gravity for CAMHS can perhaps be seen as shifting subtly from health to the local authority, represented by education and social services. Primary health care and, particularly, general practice, although acknowledged in the NSF as part of a comprehensive CAMHS, may miss out as a result, despite the fact that about one third of consultations involve children and about a quarter of those children have psychological problems (Garralda & Bailey, 1986) and may be frequent attenders (Garralda, Bowman, & Mandalia, 1999). It is timely to be reminded in the NSF that problems encountered in primary care are not necessarily less complex or less serious than those seen at other levels.

Many of the arguments proposed at the time for setting up a family therapy clinic in a large group general practice remain relevant today. Referrals to specialist CAMHS services from primary health care often fail to materialize, and it is likely that referrals from other non-medical settings in the community will experience similar difficulties. Problems with local services, particularly in child psychiatry and in psychotherapy, continue to make such help difficult and, at times, impossible to obtain locally. The belief that families would find it easier to attend their local GP practice rather than a CAMHS clinic appear to have been borne out, and there has been at least the opportunity of working in more preventative ways before problems become intractable. It is not yet clear that schools and children's centres, for example, will be more acceptable venues for mental health intervention. Meanwhile, the support and encouragement of the GP partners and other members of the primary care team, which was so important in creating the context for the establishment of the clinic, survives in the face of many organizational and political pressures. This suggests perhaps that where the fit is good between the users of services—in this case, both families and referrers—and the providers, the service itself can prosper and develop.

Where does a family clinic fit in?

The Children's NSF quotes an earlier government document, *Improvement, Expansion and Reform* (Department of Health, 2002), which indicates that a comprehensive CAMHS should be available in all areas by 2006. In spite of this, it still remains the case that while Tier 1 services, including primary care, are acknowledged, there are few convincing models to guide these services. Those models that do exist differ greatly in terms of the skills and training of the workers as well as in their location (primary or secondary) and in the emphasis of their work (direct or mainly consultation/ liaison or training/supervision).

In the family clinic, we have wondered from time to time about the tiered model, and where we fit within it. We have generally described our work to others as occupying "the interface between Tiers 1 and 2", but this is not always the case. At one stage, for example, we received an unusually large number of referrals of adolescents with early-onset eating disorders, and we became, for a while, a "mini" specialist service in a primary care setting. Like general practice itself, we are at times all things to all people.

What we hold to be distinct from the models currently being proposed is a refusal to adhere to demarcations that come from secondary care. We have no age cut-off and are as happy to see families with disruptive toddlers as couples in their eighties seeking marital therapy. Is this important? We think so, because this is how primary care works. It deals with unselected distress, and although much categorization is helpful, in this arena it often is not. Recently, McDaniel (2004) has described "medical family therapy"—perhaps a useful designation for the work of the family clinic—as a "metaframework which seeks to enhance agency and communion, while restoring hope and inspiration for patients, families, and health professionals . . . who face the physical emotional ethical and financial adversities of our day". Much of the frustration that GPs feel towards mental health services relates to the ways in which the needs of the service often seem to define access. We believe that we continue to provide a much-valued service for our practice precisely because we fit with the context of primary care. We continue to see the families referred by our colleagues without selection, but the flavour of the work has changed over time. This presumably is in response to our own development and that of our colleagues, as well as being linked to developments "out there" in terms of the availability of other services.

In response to external political demands and pressures, we have extended the model of the clinic into an outreach service. However, we have tried to remain true to our general practice roots by being flexible, collaborative, and responsive to both patients and referrers in ways that defy certain attempts at categorization. Such a service forms a small but significant part of the local mental health provision. We would want to argue not for the "rolling out" of this particular kind of systemic clinic to other areas, but for the development, through training, supervision, and support, of other perhaps similar initiatives, designed to fit the particular context. Our belief is that one size will not fit all. We continue to be involved with families who share with us many different stories of change, adversity, and strength, and we have been privileged to help where we can.

CHAPTER FIVE

Supervision and general practice: towards a reflecting position

Sara Barratt

I work as a systemic psychotherapist in general practice. Over many years, I have developed different ways of working with my medically trained colleagues, often based on the concept of supervision. For systemic therapists, supervision is a familiar part of training, even though the opportunities for live supervision may dwindle as trained staff members are employed in secondary services. For doctors, neither live nor reported supervision are part of the accepted working practice. In addition, the word "supervision"—especially among doctors—often implies a higher level of knowledge. I therefore prefer to think of supervision in terms of professional collaboration. Collaborative work in general practice—between therapist, GP, and client—can over time provide an added dimension to the relationship between doctor and patient. Rolland (1998) and Blount and Bayona (1994) emphasize the importance of interdisciplinary teams working collaboratively to generate new descriptions for patients in their cultural and life contexts, stressing the importance for patients of integrating the psychosocial and biological aspects of their lives. Collaborating by generating different perspectives on which the patient has the opportunity to comment provides the opportunity for professionals to attend to the affect of their deliberations and to learn from the patient.

There have been important developments in creating structures for evaluating and reflecting on inter-agency and interdisciplinary clinical practice (Malterud & Kristiansen, 1995). There may also be an assumption that supervision ought to be the same across different agencies. However, Storm and Todd (2001) suggest that it is important for supervision to be consistent with the needs of the context and the patients. Life in general practice is reactive to patient demand, so formulating structures for providing supervision can be difficult to achieve. Supervision can therefore take many forms: for example, corridor conversations about patients who have just been seen, or requests from GPs for advice about how to respond to requests for physical investigations of symptoms (when the GP is convinced these are contextual in origin), and opportunities to talk about the distress that members of the practice team feel when a much-loved long-term patient has a life-threatening illness.

Harré (1986) describes the cultural relativity of emotion, defining "felt states" that are related to the physical conditions of life; for those living in cultural contexts that do not have the space for emotion, the GPs we consult may see emotions manifested in physical symptoms and will debate how best to talk to the patient about a secondary referral. Such referrals require a decision by the GP about whether the most useful "treatment" is a physical or a psychological intervention, and also whether a referral to a mental health professional outside the practice is appropriate. As a therapist in general practice such distinctions are less important, and patients may be willing to see me because a referral to someone working at the surgery does not carry the stigma of a referral to a secondary mental health service. This also means that the distinction between supervision and clinical work is less clear than it might be with an outside professional.

A collaborative approach

In what follows I describe a method of collaborative supervision developed by myself and a GP colleague—Jack Czauderna, working in Sheffield and using a "reflecting team" model (Andersen, 1987, 1990). Our work was influenced by the ideas of Graham et al. (1992) who developed a family therapy clinic within a GP surgery in which GPs and therapists worked together to create a clinical supervision team. Our work was mainly with individuals; the model provides an opportunity for the therapist to be present in the room and to reflect with the GP on their relationship with the patient, mainly *during the consultation itself.* As the therapist, I reflect in front of the patient on my thoughts about what I have heard during the consultation and talk with the GP about his reflections, so that the patient hears two levels of reflection. The aim is to be tentative rather than prescriptive and to draw on personal and professional experience rather than a means of delivering advice. The GP–patient relationship is usually ongoing: it continues until one moves away. So the role of the supervisor is to provide an interruption or punctuation to the relationship. The challenge for therapist and doctor is to have a conversation between them to stimulate curiosity and creativity.

The decision to work together was largely pragmatic. We were interested in using the difference that came from our professional backgrounds and thinking to provide a new dialogue in the consulting-room. Our model of working came out of conversations about the different perspectives of the GP and therapist. We felt that it would be helpful to use those differences in approach and in task. When someone sees a psychotherapist, they have already accepted the notion that their problem may have a psychological basis. When consulting a GP, patients come with undifferentiated problems; they are often looking for physical causes and do not engage in the idea that their symptoms may be systemic rather than organic in origin. We therefore thought we would work together as reflecting supervisor and GP to engage in conversations in front of the patient in which we discussed our different ways of seeing the patient's dilemma.

We decided that I would join a morning surgery every two weeks. Patients arranging appointments for that day were told that I would be there and had the option to arrange appointments for different times if they were not comfortable with my presence. Before the appointment—alone with the GP—the patient again had the option to ask that I leave; a consent form is signed for video recording. In the consultation, the patient was told that I was visiting and that we sometimes worked together. After initial introductions I would sit facing Jack to avoid eye contact with the patient and wait until Jack invited me to give my opinion. We then conducted a conversation in front of the patient about the ideas we each had had during the consultation and how things could be different.

Over time we attracted regulars who found the joint approach useful and would return for the Monday surgeries when I was there. In the regular morning surgery we saw eleven or twelve patients who included people of all ages with ailments, such as sore throats and joint pain, but of whom more than half usually came to talk about symptoms that were related to their environment, such as psychosomatic ailments or depression. The GP also arranged half-hour slots for individuals, couples, or families with whom he felt that he was stuck and that he would benefit from a consultation.

About 40% of patients in the surgery are from the Pakistani, Bangladeshi, Somali, and Yemeni communities, and the GP also provides a service to the "traveller" community living locally. There are high levels of deprivation and poverty, which lead to high consultation rates to general practitioners. As a white British southern therapist I tried to maintain an awareness of the different cultural contexts that influenced my perceptions, in terms of the use of non-medical language and systemic ideas delivered with a southern accent. I was aware of the possible dissonance between my delivery and the way it was received. I always had to keep in mind the question: "How can I be different enough but not too different from the doctor and his patients?" The following case study shows how we work and the kind of effect this can have.

Case study: "Len"

Len, a 70-year-old white British taxi driver, consulted for extreme pain in his thigh and knee. He had been referred for investigations of other pains and was told that the results of the x-rays were negative and that there was nothing wrong. On this occasion, after a physical examination, Len recounted all the things that he used to do to keep fit that he could do no longer do. Jack turned to me, saying that he was puzzled by Len's problems.

Here are some extracts from the conversation that followed. (This is a verbatim report of the consultation. Some contextual facts have been distorted to ensure confidentiality. "Len" has been pleased to give written permission for this extract to be published.)

JC: For periods of time he seems OK, then comes with this sort of story: pain, sometimes in a different place—with pain which is really difficult for doctors, hospitals, and us here to really put our fingers on. . . . Now they've done some X-rays: special X-rays to see if they can find it . . . but it's never clear-cut. . . . And he's been depressed before as well, and the relationship between when the pain comes—wherever it is—however poorly we can understand it from a medical point of view. . . . I've never been able to quite fit it into whatever else is going on in his life.

SB: Do you ask?

JC: Not always, because it's always so focused on the pain. So it's something I need to be able to do—and need to come to some arrangement about it. When I see his wife, she's sometimes been quite low herself. Some of that has been worry and concern about Len.

SB: Because he's depressed?

JC: Because he's either depressed or he's got pain.

SB: I wondered, because one of the things we know is that people who are keen to keep themselves fit . . . it's a very good antidote to depression.

JC: Oh, yes.

SB: So, if keeping fit is about keeping on top of things—and I don't know if you think he puts pressure on himself to keep young and keep on top of things—perhaps when he doesn't, it's that much more of a disaster for him than for people who don't work as hard. And perhaps it connects with depression because being energetic helps people to battle against it.

JC: It ties in with pain also, because people do have aches and pains in life. If things are going OK, they are able to do it—cope with it—in any way they can. And then if they are not, the whole possibility that they aren't going to be as active as they were just adds in. People really feel that in their bodies rather than in their feelings and their emotions. So there is a tie in there for me, but it's always difficult for me to move into talking about what else is going on.

SB: Hmm.

JC [to Len]: Does any of that make sense?

Len: The most depressing part is not being able to do it—to cut back and cut back. You watch the young ones and what they are doing: the higher weights than what you are doing. And the weights you are lifting drop back. That's why I prefer training by myself.

JC: Do you? Is there any connection between when you feel like that—the depression—and when you get the pain?

Len: No, because certain people fifteen to twenty years younger than me—people aged fifty-five—I'm not competing with them. I train on my own.

JC turns to SB.

SB: I'm not completely convinced—he may not be competing with them, but he's very aware of what they are up to! [*Laughter*]

Len: When I'm too much aware of it, I walk out of that gym and go to another one on my own.

After this appointment, Jack reported that he was able to use the information from this consultation to draw on all aspects of Len's life in their work together. Len apparently became interested in noticing the relationship between his physical health and depression. Six weeks after the consultation above, Len attended a hospital outpatient's clinic. The letter from the consultant stated: "This gentleman was in very good spirits today. He tells me he is feeling champion and is back to his normal exercise programme. He still has occasional mild ache in the right groin but feels this is probably related to his hip as it stiffens if he sits for long periods."

According to Jack's account, the nature of Len's problems changed after this. He has never returned to the same symptom pattern as before. When symptoms do not seem to fit with pathology, Jack has found it easy to have a conversation about this and use the consultation session described above to weave together life narrative, family, and emotional factors. For example, Len developed different symptoms some time after the consultation session, and I saw him with his wife and returned to some of the issues previously discussed. One such session was enough for him to lose a whole collection of symptoms. Most other consultations are appropriate problems for general practice. Jack says he has been able to reflect with Len on issues that connect to his life story, and both GP and patient learned to talk about these in the supervised session.

The reflecting team

The idea of the reflecting team was developed from the work of Peggy Papp and Olga Silverstein (Papp, 1983), who, as family therapists, would involve the team in a debate about their different perceptions in front of the family they were seeing. Tom Andersen (1987, 1990) used these ideas as a basis for his use of a reflecting team. The purpose of sharing ideas in front of patients is that they are more transparent, and the patient's feedback contributes to an emerging new conversation between the people involved. It is important to use respectful language and to talk together in a way that attends to the complexity of the patient's situation while understanding the predicament.

The place of the reflecting supervisor is to introduce optimism that the patient has the competence to make changes. Merl (1995) lists four rules for the reflecting team, the first three based on Andersen's (1987) model:

1. Reflect only about what you have noticed, seen and felt in the session.

2. Reflect about it in a hypothetical way, leaving room for doubt or rejection.

3. Reflect about it in a benevolent manner, always looking for underlying good intentions, even if outcomes are bad.

The fourth rule is based on De Shazer's (1985) ideas:

4. Give credit to clients for what appears useful in the direction of the desired outcome and praise them for their achievements.

Merl says:

> The first three rules help clients to accept new ideas on how things could be or could turn out, without losing their competence and responsibility for their lives. The fourth rule creates and/or reinforces the client's feeling of being basically competent. [p. 49]

For the reflecting supervisor in general practice the use of non-medical language is important. So is the introduction of ideas about the patient's life outside the consulting-room, attending to areas of life in which the patient may feel competent. It helps to start the reflecting conversation by introducing mention of significant relationships in the patient's personal life and amplifying this as the consultation proceeds. For a GP who is stuck with repeated presentations of symptoms and demands for treatment, such ideas from the supervisor session can be used in subsequent consultations as a way of introducing optimism and amplifying competencies that the patient may have started to develop.

Often the purpose of a patient's consultation to a general practitioner is to try to find an explanation for a problem—and the explanation is expected to solve the problem. However, as Tom Andersen (2004) says: "any description can only be one of many descriptions". Andersen argues that we first notice something or other (in other words, we make a distinction), so we pay attention only to that one part of what is being said, and we turn away from other things that the person is saying. As doctors or as therapists, the distinctions we make are determined by our professional training and personal and professional experiences. When we talk, the first person we talk to is ourselves. Our listeners will also listen to what we have to say from the position of what they have come to hear. With all conversations between people, our ability to hear and to recall is determined by the limits of our experiences.

For myself and for the colleague I work with, we have found that we can learn a great deal by listening through the ears of the other. In all communications we will hear some things and ignore or not hear others. As therapists, we will listen to and hear the story of a relationship; we may also be attuned to listening to the meanings of illness both from different cultural perspectives and from the perspective of family and wider systems (Kleinman, 1988). As medically trained practitioners, by contrast, we will focus mainly on the story of physical symptoms in what we can hear. Our professional and cultural backgrounds, and the exploration of differences in our beliefs, can provide a tension that adds an extra dimension to our work.

As doctor and therapist, we are both aware of the way that power affects the way we listen and are listened to. Therapists in general practices have the opportunity to widen the focus from talking about symptoms to talking about the context for the symptoms. There is time to take feedback from patients and work cooperatively to develop new narratives. However, for all of us there is a danger of getting so excited by our own ideas that we leave our clients behind, feeling misunderstood and silenced. This is true in all medical and therapeutic work. When doctors work alone, there is a danger of closing down—or of "knowing" what is going on. The doctor gets into a comfortable position as expert knower. The power relationship also determines the ears through which the doctor is heard. The presence of another person changes the way both doctor and patient think about themselves in the relationship. However, the ideas presented by the supervisor are also inevitably heard in the context of the perceived power relationship between doctor and patient, and between doctor and "supervisor".

At the same time, the presence of two reflecting professionals opens up the possibility for both of being in a relationship with another rather than holding on to the idea of knowing. It is important to remember that the power that two professionals can exert over a patient in a GP consultation can be huge, and this always needs to be attended to. Gender issues are also important here, and sometimes we use our gender difference to present the different experiences of men and women, particularly when attending to cultural issues.

Body and time

One important aspect of therapist–GP–patient collaboration is that everyone needs to find different ways of thinking about the physical. For many patients consulting a general practitioner with physical symptoms, the notion that a very real pain could have a psychological basis is puzzling. When a patient consults a doctor about a physical symptom, the notion that the prescription may be for psychotherapy rather than a chemical intervention may be difficult to hear—especially if a ten-minute consultation has only provided the opportunity to describe physical symptoms. Listening with a therapist present may open people's ears to listening in different ways.

Working alongside a medical doctor, and as a therapist who gets listened to, I try to maintain the balance between attention to the physical and to the "psychosomatic" and, in particular, to respect the patient's view of the problem. For GP consultations, the physical is always privileged over the psychological. There is an ever-present danger for doctors of missing something important. They may have to explore physical investigations even though experience tells them this may be unnecessary. For the therapist it may be the other way round, but the tension and open debate can itself provide a useful intervention for the patient.

The different time structures between the usual practice of GPs and therapists can also influence what can be heard. Therapists may listen with a view to considering what the patient can accept as a comment, knowing that there will be further opportunities to develop this at the next meeting. However, when a GP suggests that a patient should make another appointment, the focus of the next consultation may be determined by what the patient wants to talk about. The patient determines the timing of the next appointment, so topics can change, and a patient may wish to talk about more and different symptoms. The agreement for a therapist to be present with the doctor gives permission to talk about the interaction between the immediate and the long-term personal experience.

While a team that is working together can learn from experience and give feedback in ways that are useful to the patient, there is always a danger of becoming too "cosy"—of getting so interested in the ideas that are being generated that the ears of the patient are ignored. However, giving feedback to patients is an essential part of the work, and general practice can, in some ways, provide feedback in a different way to other therapeutic agencies. Patients who do not like what they hear will consult other GPs in the practice, so the team of partners and other professionals is very useful and is a resource that is not available in secondary or tertiary agencies.

The nature of general practice is such that patients may be seen frequently or rarely. For Jack, working in an area of cultural diversity with high levels of poverty and deprivation, patients consulting frequently with unexplained physical symptoms provide the greatest challenge. While I have been working with him as supervisor, we have concentrated on our work with people who present with physical symptoms and depression who have been referred to all available secondary and tertiary services and whom Jack invites for a longer appointment so that I can offer consultation to his work.

Case study: "Audrey"

Jack invited Audrey, who was a very frequent attendee, to come for a half-hour appointment.

Audrey is divorced, with five adult children and eight grandchildren. She is in a relationship with a married man whose wife is seriously ill with multiple sclerosis. Audrey became ill with pancreatitis some time ago and has, since then, developed pain and other physical symptoms that do not respond to treatment and which, for Jack, did not fit together in medical terms. He said that there was no way to categorize the difficulties that she brought, as they changed at each consultation. Jack said that he would welcome my involvement because, despite multiple referrals to secondary services, all tests returned with negative results, and Audrey wanted more investigations.

We hypothesized that Audrey's partner was managing the illness of his wife, while Audrey's own children were responsible for their own small children, so that she might only feel entitled to a relationship with them through ill health. In thinking about the contexts for her life it, was difficult to know what would encourage Audrey to develop a story for herself about health rather than illness. (This, too, is an edited and anonymized transcript; "Audrey" has given consent for publication)

Audrey came into the room, saying: "I have been in such pain, Dr Jack, I have a headache that never leaves me. My daughter will tell you that I can't get out of bed. . . ." The consultation then continued:

JC: Can I introduce you to Sara ?

Audrey: But Dr Jack, my stomach has been really bad. I think it's the cystitis but it's so bad I'm in pain all over, up my back. I can't move . . .

JC: We'll talk about this in a minute, but first I want to let you know that Sara and I sometimes work together. She's a family therapist, and I think it's helpful for her to join me to help me think about our work together.

Audrey: But Dr Jack, my legs are in such pain I can't walk. I think I need an X-ray because I don't know what it can be . . .

Jack continued to explain the way we worked together, but Audrey was so preoccupied with her different symptoms that it was hard for her to listen. Audrey was clearly distressed by her problems. Her headaches meant that she could not tolerate her grandchildren, and her family were no longer sympathetic to her. She said that she would love to spend more time with her grandchildren and take them to the park, but this was not possible. Her pain meant that she was not able to work, and she wondered if her disability allowance could be increased. Jack felt unable to help. He had carefully investigated Audrey's different symptoms, and no physical cause had been established. He turned to me and said that he was at a loss to know how to help.

Audrey listened to a conversation between us. I wondered aloud whether he thought that Audrey believed that there was nothing further that he could do and whether there may be other explanations for Audrey's pain. Jack said he thought that it might be a manifestation of her sadness. She never spoke about how she felt emotionally, but he thought that her life was quite difficult. I asked in what way, and he replied that her partner was still married, and she may feel upset that she spent so much time alone. I wondered whether her symptoms also prevented her from helping with the care of her grandchildren and being an active family member.

Jack turned to Audrey to ask what she had been thinking of when she was listening. Audrey said that she did see her grandchildren but would like to do more with them if she didn't have the pain; Jack said he was interested in the idea that she may feel sad but that she never spoke about this. Audrey did not respond to this but said she just wanted an end to the pain. Jack asked Audrey if she thought he could put an end to the pain. She said that she did not think so, but that she could not take any more.

Jack turned to me again. I said that I wondered whether she had a religious belief, or if there were other forms of help that she had tried. Jack said that Audrey had asked him about acupuncture, in a way that made him think she had a belief that this could help. Because acupuncture was only available privately, Jack had referred her to an aromatherapist who worked in the local NHS. Audrey said that she had started to go to church. Although she was not religious, she had prayed for help. I wondered if this belief would be as helpful as her belief in Jack. Jack thought this was an interesting idea. I said that I wondered if Audrey thought she could use resources within herself to relieve some of the symptoms, and whether this could be as effective as consulting him. Jack said he thought this would be worth exploring with Audrey, and he talked to her about other ideas she had for relieving her symptoms. Audrey became more engaged in this idea and felt that her connection with the church community, which re-connected her with the religion of her family of origin, might provide some comfort.

Jack has spoken to Audrey since this consultation and has written to her clarifying some issues that had come out of the collaborative consultation.

Family therapists are accustomed to writing letters between sessions to reflect on the ideas that emerged for them and to provide another context for the ongoing work. White and Epston (1989) developed a model for writing to families following sessions to build on the ideas they had developed: "persons who have virtually lost their lives to problems find it difficult to escape despair" (p. 77).

It felt as if Audrey had been unable to contemplate thoughts and emotions apart from despair. The purpose of the consultation had been for Jack to use the ideas generated in our joint meeting to bring to future consultations. We both thought it important to write with the ideas he had taken from the consultation, so Jack wrote the following letter:

> *Dear Audrey,*
>
> *First of all I'd like to thank you for allowing Sara to sit in with us last week. Her role is to help me think about how best to help you. You may have heard that one in seven of the population suffer from chronic back pain. When it is as extensive as yours it involves all parts of your body, and one pain seems to trigger others. The chronic pain includes causes like migraine, arthritis, mechanical back pain, and interstitial cystitis. One of the difficulties is that we do not have a cure for any of these conditions, and the main treatment is self-management. This means you have to find things you can do which you believe in, which suit you, and which you can do every day to get you through. This is what Sara meant when she wondered if you could find activities such as walking, exercises, things you want to do to help you feel better. You also need to do the things you believe in—religion if you do, or acupuncture, or whatever.*

So this is what I am prepared to do:

— *Help you with exercise and other activities; the pain clinic will help you with self management; it is much more likely to help with this than with injections.*

— *Refer to acupuncturist; you can talk to him about other complementary therapies, including aromatherapy.*

— *No further investigations. I have no indication for sending you for X-rays, scans, or any other investigation. These are to find the cause of the symptoms. We have not been able to find the cause, and the hope of chasing this for the rest of your life will only prolong your pain. We have to stop this now.*

— *I will support you to think about benefits, etc., but remember that, if you have to be ill to get benefits, it will be harder for you to get better.*

— *Some treatments and tablets are worth taking. The Amitriptyline, good for chronic pain, is probably worth it. Unless you have a water infection, antibiotics are no help. Painkillers for the above are not good for long-term pain.*

In the end you will need to find the supports that fit best for you in managing your pain; I'll see you soon.

Yours sincerely

Following this letter, Jack has received two telephone calls from Audrey. He says that he was able to think more carefully about his capacity, as the doctor, to find a solution to her problems. She has not consulted other doctors in the practice, and Jack feels that he is more able to give responsibility back to Audrey. He says that he has been able to change the pattern of his responses and is not as preoccupied by her as he was before the consultation. He feels that the consultation helped him to clarify what he could and could not do and that she is managing her symptoms in a new way. He says that the consultation has helped him to think differently about his work with Audrey and to clarify his thinking through writing the letter. He says that this helped him to devise a plan and, as it was in writing, stick to it.

Conclusion

The long-term nature of the relationship between GP and patient means that GPs find themselves looking to many different health resources in the hope that there will be some relief for both patient and doctor. Sometimes referrals can take place in desperation and as the hopelessness of the patients is shared among those working with them. Supervision can provide the opportunity to connect the physical and the psychological and to bring the network of family and culture into the consulting-room. For people suffering pain without physical explanation in particular, it is important that the listener understands that the pain is real and that, while the contextual factors are important, the reality of the experience is validated.

As the GP works usually with individuals and different family members consult to different GPs, it is difficult—even for systemic GPs—to bring thinking about the patient's context into the consultation. GPs work alone and, in the short space of a morning surgery, will hear a range of problems that have an emotional impact. There is little opportunity to process any but the most painful events, which may affect them. My supervision is intended to amplify the usual conversations that take place between doctor and patient. While patients with recurrent symptoms that do not change may find it hard to hear different ideas that link their physical symptoms with family concerns, the GP can use my ideas to change the nature of future conversations. Jack will no doubt continue to struggle with finding ways to help patients who have become stuck in very painful difficulties in their health and their lives and to try to manage the balance between compassion and realism in his ability to cure their ills. However, he can remember the ideas we generated in my consultation session to build on in future encounters with the patient.

It is unusual to have an opportunity to work in this way. In holding on to the difference in our knowledge base, we can each present our different experiences of what is going on. Each of us can also take the opportunity to "not know", which is an important part of our consultations. The ignorance that I bring enables me to ask naïve questions—sometimes questions that the patient feels unable to ask—that connect symptoms with my ideas about family and context. For me, as supervisor, the opportunity to hear the range of different problems that a GP encounters (and to appreciate the constraint that he is expected to know the solution) is exciting and moving.

Supervision has also been reciprocal. Jack's supervision of my own work with clients whom I have seen in the surgery has provided the opportunity for me to introduce a different perspective to my own clinical work. Clients have found this interesting too in expanding our ongoing discussions. Our consultations have, therefore, provided the opportunity for both of us to learn from one another about our different professional perspectives.

CHAPTER SIX

When the patient and family are from somewhere else: narratives of migration in therapy

Jenny Altschuler

T his chapter explores the challenges of working in primary care with large numbers of people who experience themselves as displaced, and for whom the concepts of community, home, and even family refer more to a place in the past rather than one in the present. It draws on systemic psychotherapeutic work that I did as part of a wider initiative in an inner-city primary care practice. The service involved meeting with up to three families fortnightly, followed by consulting with the medical staff on a range of issues, including discussing the families seen in therapy, patients who raised particular concerns but for whom a referral was not feasible, and wider practice issues.

Primary care: a community response

Systemic psychotherapy focuses not only individuals and families, but on their relationship to the wider context, their community. As such, it is particularly pertinent to a primary care practice with a large number of immigrant patients, placing emphasis on creating a context that is community-based (Hopkins, 2002). The practice offers a range of services, including medical consultations, and specific psychotherapeutic services, including child psychology, counselling, and family psychotherapy. In addition, a community worker coordinates liaison with the local social, education-, and health-related services, including a specific project offering women the opportunity of contributing to a gardening project. Many of those most distressed will have had experiences that have left them ambivalent about trusting figures of authority, unsure of their right to ask and receive the care they and their families need. Community outreach services are therefore crucial to ensure that people are informed of their right to access what is available.

For displaced families, medical consultations in the GP surgery can help them to experience emotional connection and establish a sense of community. Even with the use of interpreters, differences in finding a shared language or shared understanding of illness and treatment may mean that consultations do not always meet the needs of the patient: professionals may be left questioning why someone has come and what has been achieved. However, what these consultations do offer is unique: it is the opportunity of being heard, respected, and taken care of. For people living far from those they might otherwise have consulted, consultations stand "in loco" of the extended family, helping people create a link between their present and past lives. For those who experience themselves as isolated, there are few similar opportunities. One exception is school or nursery: it is only there that one can meet another adult whose role it is to hold one's child in mind, thereby standing in for those who are no longer present.

Narrative approaches

The idea of using narrative as a way of healing has always been intrinsic to psychotherapeutic work, but more recently Michael White and David Epston (1990) have developed a particular way of conceptualizing the use of narrative in an approach that places emphasis on conversations where:

- the client's experience is privileged over that of the therapist or referrer in defining the problem;

- questions are asked to separate the client from the influence of the problem story;

- emphasis is placed on exceptions: current and past experiences that contradict the problem story are noticed;

- subsequent questions explore the meaning of these less noticed experiences, with the goal of helping the client to re-author an alternative story so that it becomes more influential than the problem story (Zimmerman & Beaudoin, 2002).

Clients are capable of functioning effectively in certain contexts, but they cannot do so in situations where they are restrained by the influence of a problem story and the discourses that shape it. This approach, therefore, has much to offer families who have experienced profound disruption, for whom identity is repeatedly contested and reconfigured in the process of fitting into a situation where the physical, social, and cultural meanings of everyday living are so different.

Culture and migration

Although current thinking in mental health has begun to recognize culture as central to people's lives and relational patterns (Dwivedi, 1999; Kelleher & Hillier, 1996; Krause, 1998; Phoenix, 2002), there is still insufficient understanding of the issues that families face in migrating to the United Kingdom. Even a move that is primarily based on choice results almost inevitably in a disruption in relationships, a move away from what is known to the unknown. We all tell stories to help us make sense of experiences and to develop some sense of continuity and coherence between our past and present experiences: indeed, the desire to narrate strange experiences relates to our very real human need to be understood, both by ourselves and by others. However, on migrating, disruptions in patterns of relationship, feelings about those left behind, and the complexity of fitting in to a new country can mean that important aspects of the story are marginalized.

The decision to migrate may not have been shared. Children and partners who are forced to move as a result of others' decisions often have greater struggles in balancing their connection to the old and new country (Falicov, 1998). While raising differences between family members may seem to increase levels of distress, ignoring them will in the long run only compound problems as these differences continue to influence everyday life, but at a covert level. Exploring and sharing narratives of migration can help family members to regain a sense of agency, reconnect with aspects of their experiences that have been excluded, and regain the strengths and resources that carried them through life prior to migration.

For some, moving to Britain represents a "step up" towards greater physical and economic security. For others it is a "step down", heralding economic uncertainty, isolation, a profound experience of not belonging, and racism. The move may have been based on choice, or for social and economic reasons, or forced as a consequence of violent political events. As such it may be dominated by images of trauma, separation, and dislocation, or the hope of a new beginning. But for all, it is a "step away" into a "diasporic space" (Brah, 1996), where displacement from a place called home and the absence of certain family members has a powerful influence in moulding the narratives and subjectivities of migrants and their families.

Not all families who migrate experience difficulties: moving away can open up opportunities that might not have been available in the country of origin. How one responds to migration is inevitably influenced by the context of the host country: racism and economic difficulties compound the complexity of saying goodbye to people and places that have formed the fabric of one's life. However, where difficulties arise, sharing memories of what led to migration and of resettling in the United Kingdom, together with hopes of integrating what may be very different cultural ideas about family life, can reposition families' difficulties as part of a wider process of change. Placing the difficulties that families experience as part of a response to an unusual life event—migration—can move personal experiences into a wider context and thus offer a less pathologizing frame for exploring difficulties. Therapy then becomes a place in which "individual and collective memories collide, reassemble and reconfigure" (Brah, 1996, p. 193), enabling families to develop a greater sense of coherence and continuity and to connect with their family strengths and resilience.

Case study: "Faduma"

Faduma consulted her GP frequently with a range of concerns about her health, including stomach pain and headaches, and because her hair was falling out. As she began to develop a sense of trust, her GP encouraged her to talk about other issues she may be worried about, and over time she began to talk at a different level. She said that her son "Mohammed", aged 10, was experiencing behavioural and learning difficulties at school, and her 5-year-old daughter, "Gulten", wet herself at night. Faduma was depressed and was struggling to cope. Three years previously, the family had left Turkey, where the father, a Turkish Kurd, had been imprisoned and tortured on political grounds. Since coming to the United Kingdom, the relationship between Faduma and her husband has become increasingly difficult: although she said this had now stopped, he had been violent to her on several occasions.

As with many families in this position, migration has had a profound impact on this family's life, spanning three genera-tions (Sluzki, 1979). Children like Mohammed and Gulten have to forge their identity in a context that is different from that of their parents, devoid of their parents' rationale for leaving, so that clashes between parents and children may come to repre-sent clashes of loyalty between cultures. Even where parents support the move, migration confronts those left behind with reconstructing the patterns of their lives, with reformulating hopes and expectations for the future. Each family has its own migration narrative—of leaving their home country, the physi-cal and emotional journey, and arriving in the United Kingdom. Faduma's family, too, had faced the challenge of dismantling and reconstructing family ties, of finding ways of remaining emotionally connected across an enormous geographic distance (Fog Olwig, 1999). Lack of familiarity with the host country can mean that the support that may be available locally cannot be accessed.

The work took place at four levels: in sessions with the general practitioner, in direct work with the family carried out by me, helping the family to access local support, and individually.

a. Primary care consultations as a stage towards psychotherapy

Prior to the referral, Faduma had talked a great deal to her GP about her physical symptoms, her headaches, stomach pain, and hair loss. The work with the GP involved addressing her requests at a physical level, but also moving beyond this to conceptualizing mind and body as linked, viewing Faduma's distress as an expression of both her physical and her emotional pain. It was only after she felt her distress had been really recognized and heard that she could move on to address her emotional pain, her sadness, shame, and anxiety about her children. It was once this trust had been established that a referral to family therapy was offered with the understanding that rather than losing the ear of the general practitioner, she was being offered more of a space in which to think about the needs of herself and her family.

b. Family work

My initial intention was to meet the whole family. As the father was unwilling to attend, the work involved meetings with Faduma and her children, sessions with Faduma alone, and liaison with school. Most sessions included an interpreter as the family had limited English and I speak neither Turkish nor Kurdish. However, language provided an important theme for exploring narratives of migration.

It has often been said that language schools are filled with people who are too depressed to learn. In many ways, difficulty in learning English was part of a wider struggle about how much to embrace life in England and accept that they would not be returning. Mohammed thought that his struggle with English confirmed how stupid he was. In exploring this further, we established that as he was fluent in Turkish and Kurdish, acquiring English would mean he spoke three languages. Questioning whether anyone else in the class spoke more than one language enabled him to alter his story to seeing himself as someone bright enough to speak several languages.

Added to this, both children felt second-class. They were very aware of what they lacked in comparison with their peers and that they had little knowledge of their family's history or their Kurdish heritage to counter this. To protect their children, Faduma and her husband seemed to have downplayed their cultural and family heritage in the hope of easing their assimilation. Although tied to their cultural past, they did not speak about it. This had the effect of distancing the children from the very people who could help them make sense of distressing experiences, their parents, unwittingly increasing the sense of difference they experienced in relation to their peers. We therefore spent time exploring how Mohammed and Gulten could learn about their heritage from speaking to their parents.

Finding words that conveyed similar meanings in English and Turkish was but one part of the process (Raval, 1996). The work also included thinking carefully about what we did and did not share. Appelfeld (2001) suggests that sometimes the only way one can truly hear is to acknowledge the differences between the speaker's world and that of the listener, to acknowledge both the unbridgeable gap between the two worlds and assimilating the impact of this unbridgeable difference. Although both the interpreter and I had migrated to the United Kingdom, our circumstances were very different, and it was important to recognize this in developing trust. As the interpreter was Turkish and the family had migrated on political grounds, we needed to think about how this influenced what might feel safe to say. Addressing these issues meant that we moved between the personal and professional in reflecting on our work together, introducing a different sense of authenticity into the work.

Difficulties were primarily lodged in Mohammed, who was seen as disrespectful to his mother. He seemed to be caught up in the conflict between his parents, moving between acting as his mother's saviour and being aggressive towards her, modelling himself on his father. Trying to free him from fighting a battle that did not belong to him included tracking the difficulties he and his mother were experiencing and looking beyond this for exceptions to narratives of arguing. This included thinking about what Faduma and others really valued about her son, and exploring what they enjoyed doing together. This allowed a quite different conversation to take place, opening up the possibility of discussing how she might be able to help him with school.

Having established greater trust, we were able to think about the bedwetting. Faduma expressed her mounting anger and frustration with wet sheets and pyjamas, while Gulten looked embarrassed and talked about how nothing had helped. In order to help them move on, the symptoms were moved from being seen as part of Gulten to something outside of her that at times could exert control over her life. Externalizing the symptoms and naming them as "trouble" enabled us to establish the times when she was able to defeat "trouble" and explore what needed to happen for this to increase, moving mother and daughter from a position of helplessness to feeling more in control. Fairly soon, they were able to beat the wetting together. This enabled us to think about being in control at a different level: bedwetting had begun soon after the children had seen their father hitting their mother, so these conversations moved on to thinking about how both Faduma and her children could ensure they remained safe.

c. Community work

School offered another context in which Faduma experienced herself and her children as being cared for. Although she could not speak English, she collected her children each day: she would greet the teachers, but lack of English meant she could not communicate with them.

This interchange seemed to play an important part of her day, yet when a school meeting with an interpreter was set up, fairly early in the work, neither parent attended. The staff initially viewed the parents' absence as evidence of their lack of interest and of their inability to meet the needs of their children. However, this event gave us an opportunity to reflect more widely, linking the academic difficulties the children were experiencing with why it may be difficult for the parents to attend such meetings. This led to a different conversation about what support the school could offer, resulting in planning for ways of developing stronger links with the parents and increasing language tuition for the children.

d. Individual work

The term, "ambiguous loss" has been used to represent the experience of migration, of being physically absent but remaining an emotional presence (Boss, 1991; Falicov, 1998). Although Faduma was physically present, sadness and ambivalence about her family back home meant that she was often emotionally absent to her children. She felt isolated and ashamed of her life. Exploring the influence migration had on her life led to thinking what her mother and siblings would say if they knew she was suffering alone. To protect herself and her family from the pain of being apart, she had cut herself off from the support of talking to her mother on the phone, or even holding on to her image as a resource. At one level, reflecting more about her family put Faduma in touch with a deep sadness, and there were times when she was very tearful. However, hypothesizing about her family helped her to draw on them as a stronger supportive mental presence, ultimately enabling her to re-establish contact with her family abroad.

When the interpreter did not arrive for a session, Faduma chose to speak for herself. Although her words were extremely halting, she used the time to share traumatic aspects of her past that she had previously chosen to keep secret. Communicating without relying on an intermediary had a profound impact on our interaction. Speaking in a language that was different from the one in which Faduma had experienced such trauma seemed to offer her some containment, so that the experiences felt less overwhelming. However, as importantly, lack of a shared language placed us on a more equal basis, forcing us both to use nonverbal communication and resulting in a more intimate process of connection.

No doubt, the work would have been different had the father agreed to participate; it might have enabled different conversations about fathering to take place. Like many couples in exile, loss of family and friendship networks seemed to have forced this isolated and marginalized couple to look to each other to make up for what had been lost. Unemployment and differences in gendered roles in the United Kingdom had exacerbated the tension they experienced, forcing them into a level of closeness that felt intolerable. This may well have contributed to precipitating incidents of violence (Agger, 1994). However, despite this, the family were able to use this context to develop an alternative story of their lives. Feedback from the GP is that the children are managing better at school, Gulten's bedwetting has not recurred, and the mother seems to be less depressed and attends the surgery less frequently than before.

Conclusions

In recent years there has been an increase in the number of refugees coming to Britain. Although many adapt well to the transitions imposed by such a move, others find themselves struggling to adapt to their altered circumstances and turn to one of the few services open to people in such distress: GP surgeries and health centres. This means that primary care staff are increasingly faced with people who come from elsewhere, people with whom they do not have a shared language or understanding of illness and treatment. Sitting with a woman who describes body pains according to parameters that do not fit with Western medical training can leave professionals feeling frustrated, deskilled, or that they have been inappropriately used. Moreover, the work takes longer and requires negotiation with interpreting and advocacy agencies.

However, holding on to the theme of migration can offer a framework for conceptualizing both the challenges and the professional opportunities introduced by this work. It offers a framework for rethinking ideas of illness as culturally constructed, repositioning the link between physical and emotional pain. Recognizing the importance of migration requires a re-conceptualization of primary care as the key to helping people risk seeking connection and acceptance, a springboard towards recreating a sense of community.

To help people recreate this sense of community means connecting our own narratives with the people we see (Altschuler, 1997). In an age in which not only those who have migrated feel displaced, recognizing the importance of the primary care team operating "in loco" the extended family offers a framework for understanding the needs of other "frequent consulters". Medical consultations become a way of establishing alternate forms of reconnection when the ties that bond have broken.

CHAPTER SEVEN

Cross-cultural work in the community

Nasima Hussain

Working in the Bangladeshi/Asian service at the Tavistock Clinic has raised a number of challenges. One of these has been to explore the possibilities of working within cultures and across cultures. Another has been how to juxtapose multiple systems, such as the clinic and the community, and how to address the dilemma of concentrating on clinic-based work versus community work. The biggest challenge has been to search for a good fit between theory, practice, and the context in which clinical work can best flourish.

As a Bangladeshi family therapist, I hold both an insider and an outsider position. I see myself as an insider, as I have a cultural and linguistic match with the families; I am also an outsider because of my within-culture differences, my education, class, and "Western" theoretical framework. This dual position has posed various challenges to my therapeutic manoeuvrability. As a Bangladeshi family therapist, it has sometimes been difficult for me to grasp concepts from within the culture. I have some ideas of the family's religious and cultural beliefs, the common understandings that the family and I share to create our therapeutic relationship, but sometimes this is not sufficient to tease out new meanings or help create an alternative story. Then the rhetoric of deconstructing the family's stories creates multiple problems in practice, exasperated as I sometimes am by what I see as within-culture similarities, such as the same religion, language, and so on.

In this chapter I discuss the dilemmas of working as a systemic family therapist with the Bangladeshi community, and the limits and possibilities of clinical outreach work in the community setting. Using a case vignette, I explore how meanings are generated in clinical work through different narratives in different contexts. I focus on themes such as illness, marriage, the role of children in the family, and the extended family, together with therapeutic issues such as empathy, mutuality, and power in cross-cultural work. I examine how I move as a therapist between two languages and two discourses: discourses arising from the therapist's Western theoretical framework and the family's own understanding of their presenting problems.

The Bangladeshi/Asian service

A service for Bangladeshi children and families at the Tavistock Clinic was originally set up in 1996, following a needs analysis. It was apparent that there was a large Bangladeshi child and adolescent population in Camden needing a mental health service, but very few families were referred to the Clinic or engaged with the service. In Camden as a whole there were no ethnically matched statutory services for this population. The Bangladeshi service was therefore set up to address a problem of accessibility and the availability of services to ethnic minority communities.

The service, based in the Child and Family department, addressed this accessibility through employing two part time clinicians—a systemic psychotherapist and a clinical psychologist. Both were Bangladeshis providing both clinic-based and outreach assessment and treatment in Bengali. The clinicians were based in a multidisciplinary team and had access to other assessment and treatment models together with colleague support and supervision. As part of the thinking about the accessibility of the service, networking was done with the community at large, including service users and providers, in order to increase referrals to the Bangladeshi service and make CAMHS more accessible to this community. The service has now been expanded into a wider Asian service, with several additional staff members speaking other south Asian languages.

Working with Bangladeshi families

Almost all the Bangladeshi families that are referred to the service are from the north-eastern region of Bangladesh called Sylhet, which has a distinctive regional identity in terms of local dialect and religion. Although Bangladesh is predominantly an open secular society, in Sylhet Islam as a religion plays a central role is family life. This is not surprising, as Islam came to the region with the help of the renowned Sufi [Islamic term for saint] Shah Jalal, whose shrine still exists in Sylhet town and is a sacred place for all Muslims. For the families in Britain, life is conducted through religious beliefs and values. Sylhet has had a long tradition of migrants and entrepreneurs, and the majority of Sylhetis in Britain are economic migrants from rural districts, with little education either in Bengali or in English. The case is different for the Bangladeshis from other districts, who, although in some ways also economic migrants, came primarily with professional qualifications or for further education.

Most of the families I see have been survivors: from hardship, poverty, displacement, and loss through the process of migration. We are aware that migration creates diasporas, and the multiple losses impact on psychological health (Brah, 1996, Pawliuk, Grizenko, Chan-Yip, Gantous, Mathew, & Nguyen, 1996, Sluzki, 1979). In honouring their experiences, one brings forth their migration stories, family-of-origin stories, and stories of their pain and suffering. These stories help them to create their personal meaning. I, as the listener, make the connection between the past and the present, watching family scripts being formulated, observing resilience, seeing their limitations and possibilities.

In understanding a problem or distress, almost always I find that families turn to their religious or cultural understanding of the problem. While that seems a natural response, it also becomes difficult for any other understanding of the problem to be put forward. I then end up with competing stories: my own hypothesis versus the family's understanding of the problem. I often find that through their religious beliefs they have externalized the problem by leaving it in "God's hand", as most families would say. This can lead to a struggle for ownership of the story: my understanding of the problem versus the family's. My own story of the problem competes for space, thus making the matrix more complex. This adds further complexities to the therapeutic process. We might think that working with the religious or cultural beliefs they present may be easier, but I often find that the families' own religious or cultural stories also start to change. Their narratives are juxtaposed: what seems their old religious understanding and their new acculturalized version. This often feels like a moving object, creating competing stories and sometimes placing the family into a confusing state.

Case study: "Juned"

Juned (aged 8) and his family were referred by the local community psychology service. Concerns were about his behaviour and learning difficulties. It seemed that his mother was having difficulty managing his behaviour and was constantly asking for help. The GP who made the original referral to the psychologist also said that there were complex family problems. Father was not with the family, and there was a history of domestic violence. The GP said that she was not able to understand fully what was happening in this family: Mrs "Begum" (the mother) spoke only Bengali, and using interpreters was not satisfactory. The psychologist who first saw Juned did psychometric tests to assess Juned's learning difficulties and liaised with his school for additional educational support. She also tried various behavioural techniques, but Mrs Begum was not able to use them. Juned's older brother "Karim" (aged 10) was doing well, and there seemed no concern about him.

I started to see the family at home; this is our usual practice, since most of the families cannot attend the Tavistock Clinic as it is too far for them and difficult to get to. There are also cultural reasons: women do not usually attend appointments by themselves, they are escorted by their husbands, and also they do not speak very much English or venture out of their area.

I have been seeing the family for over a year, providing 20 sessions at fortnightly to monthly intervals. Some of the sessions were with Camden social services as part of their child-in-need assessment. The sessions were mainly with the mother and the two boys, and sometimes with the mother alone. The extended family members did not wish to participate in the sessions and would leave when I visited.

Mrs Begum soon began to tell me in Bengali about her health problems and her domestic problems. She talked of the pains in various parts of her body. She talked about the state of her housing situation, and she told me that her ex-husband had been violent towards her from the beginning of their marriage. She told me due to his violence that she had attempted suicide when she was pregnant with Juned. Since then she had successfully divorced her husband with the support of her extended family. However, he still continued to harass her through the community by hiring various people to telephone her in the middle of the night, burgle her house, bang on her window, and so on. She had reported this to the police, but no one had been charged.

From the beginning what seemed clear was that Mrs Begum has much physical pain, which became a recurring theme in the sessions. She talked about having pain in her back similar to her sister, who had died of a cancer a few months earlier, and with each pain there was a story of a family member who had suffered. She had had many physical investigations, but no diagnosis. She continued to go to her GP almost every week, who had become impatient with her. Other simultaneous themes were of housing and social problems, the difficulty of raising children—especially boys—without a father, and the loneliness of being out of a marriage.

Core themes

A number of core themes—family, marriage, and illness—came up in the therapy.

Family

In my sessions, I established the supportive role that the extended family has been playing for Mrs Begum and the children— this included aunts, uncles, and grandparents. In so doing, I recognized that the mother–child dyad was not necessarily the most significant dyad. In this case, some aspects of the child's needs were met through the extended family. Mother's commitment to keeping a connection with her family in Bangladesh has shown the boys that they have other support. This reciprocated bond has allowed the children's needs to be thought about and nurtured in the family. I learned that aunts and uncles would visit regularly, and the boys had regular telephone conversations with maternal grandmother in Bangladesh.

Commentary: Perhaps in a Western context it may be expected that the child's needs are met mainly through a one-to-one connection with a parent, usually the mother. In the Bangladeshi context this could be seen as individualistic, as the child would almost always be part of a wider system of kinship structures. During my clinical work with Bangladeshi families I observed that children's emotional issues are not necessarily given precedence. This does not imply that children in such families are not emotionally nurtured but, rather, that families present with complex beliefs around children's emotional worlds. One such belief may come from the fact that Bangladeshi families have a hierarchical structure in which the child subsystem is at the bottom of the hierarchy. Thus, children's emotional needs are often submerged within the collective structure of the family, with their physical needs receiving more attention. This is also true for adults' emotional needs. The structure shifts the focus away from the individual, thus making it less overt. The self is relational and not individualistic. Emotional needs are then not expressed overtly. This may give rise to somatization. In practice, the complexity lies in translating the somatization back to the family in an emotional framework.

Marriage

I started to ask Mrs Begum questions that pieced together her marriage story. She told me that her father, who was an educated and open-minded man, had arranged this marriage. She had a lot of good positive memories of her father, and I realized that she held him as a role model. This was posed as an alternative story to her experience of her husband, and we were able to acknowledge where her strength came from as a single mother.

Commentary: In practice, it is often helpful to think about how the meaning of marriage is constructed and held by individuals. This can be seen in terms of stories stemming from their families of origin, religion, culture, and society. From a social constructionist position, the therapist can then challenge the assumed and taken-for-granted meaning of marriage, with an awareness that these meanings are embedded in history and culture. Because knowledge and meanings are constructed in the interactions between people, "storying" and "re-authoring" the story is a way to "co-construct" possibilities for change.

My understanding of the significance of marriage, and of the meaning attached to it in the Bangladeshi culture, comes from my shared knowledge, cultural familiarity, and personal and professional experience. This positions me as insider and outsider simultaneously. A finely honed and intuitive sense of both the "insider" and "outsider" positions that I hold as a Bangladeshi therapist working with Bangladeshi families creates possibilities for what can and cannot be said. For example, with Bangladeshi families it is often difficult and delicate to raise issues of separation and divorce, ideas that are often loaded with shame and guilt.

Illness

Illness is another dominant and powerful part of the narrative that I have observed in most of my cases. It always makes me ask the question, "What function does the illness serve in the system?" In the majority of cases it has been difficult to shift this narrative. Most of the families that I see are in the poverty trap, with very little education and socioeconomic prospects. The illness serves the function of a voice in which help can be sought. It also plays an important function in expressing the desires of the relational self in the collective family structure. Because the self is relational and culturally an individual's desire is not sought overtly, the illness acts to express the individual's inner needs and keeps it focused through the narrative. This narrative becomes part of the homeostasis—the self regulating system. Shifting this becomes difficult, as there would be a void if the narrative were shifted.

Issues for the therapist

As well as the themes we explored in the therapy, there were a number of therapeutic issues for me to think about or to negotiate: language, power, mutuality, and empathy.

Language is always an important aspect of the therapeutic relationship. Bilingualism adds to the fluidity of moving between the positions of insider and outsider, allowing me to transport meaning from one context to another. It helps me in engaging and facilitating the therapeutic relationship. Sharing a language with the family can be a fast entry point into the joining process. With shared cultural understanding being another important level, the matched cultural identity and language is a definite advantage. However, it is also possible to work with families without speaking the same language so long as this is facilitated by good cultural understanding.

The dynamics of power and authority are always a central theme in the therapy process. The client is aware of the therapist's power, and the therapist may be aware of belonging to a dominant group and deriving power from multiple sources. This power is needed not to gratify the therapist but to regulate the social relationship. In this case power issues were explored covertly through the client being curious about my age and family structure, in order to place me within my own family hierarchy. While this kind of interchange may be problematic in some other settings, with Bangladeshi clients there is for me a recursive relationship between empathy for the client and my expert knowledge. From the outset, I am always aware of hierarchy in the relationship, and I work towards fitting it in and addressing it, as opposed to trying to equalize it. This issue then becomes more available for both the therapist and client to address.

Mutuality in therapy is the idea that both client and therapist regulate each other in the working alliance. Here, the Asian concept of the "relational" self plays a central role in the therapy process and its outcome. In Asian cultures the self is seen as more relational, as opposed to individualistic. This means that an individual's actions and behaviour are more dependent on thought for others and focused more in the collective and social arena. My relational self as a Bengali has been culturally constructed so as to be able to express mutuality through verbal and nonverbal communications. Sometimes this nonverbal communication remains at the unconscious level. At the same time, exploring and finding difference is an important aspect of therapy. This brings challenges in trying to separate therapist from client. In my work with Asian/ Bangladeshi clients, my similarity helps me to join with them. My own need to fit in, and to maintain harmonious connections with the client, are helpful in the therapy process. However, the advantage of joining easily with my clients through our common relational selves—and the knowledge of how these facilitate the therapy—sometimes makes it difficult to see, create, and maintain differences, and it requires a conscious effort in the therapeutic process to do so.

In Asian cultures empathy is necessary to reinforce harmony. According to Ham (1993), empathy in the West is a taught skill, whereas in Asian cultures it is part of traditional philosophy and religious systems. Roland (1991) states that empathy in the therapeutic relationship with South Asian clients is expressed by the therapist's caring and nurturing role. The ability to empathize with the client is shown through nonverbal communication and through providing advice. The skills of paying attention and empathetic listening are required in order to establish trust and a positive therapeutic relationship.

In the above case empathy was facilitated by the similarity of language, culture, and race. Knowing the intricate details of Bengali family life also allowed me to be in an empathetic position. Yet similarity was both a positive and negative experience. For example, I needed to convince the family of confidentiality, as I could be seen as too close to the community to be trusted. The boundary of the client–therapist relationship was often stretched, as my empathetic position encouraged curiosity from the client.

Mrs Begum would often ask about my own experiences of negotiating my Bengali family life. This forced me to take a "meta position" and reframe to her some of my own reflections on illnesses and pain in family life, then exploring with her the similarities and differences that we shared. I would often put this in the context of my observation of Bangladeshi families and the difficulties they faced in Britain. For example, in one session we talked about the role of Bengali women and her struggle as a single parent/mother. She asked whether I had a family in London, and I said yes. This curiosity did not go further. I then gave her examples of other single parents and mothers with whom I had worked and how they managed and then asked her what her views were. She found this most valuable and seemed contained by the thought of others having problems.

Conclusion

Cross-cultural work poses many theoretical and practice challenges, pushing us to explore alternative ways of thinking about our work. These include thinking about the theoretical boundaries of psychotherapy models, opening the debate to questions such as the following: Can there be a good fit between Western models of psychotherapy and clients from minority ethnic groups? How can we find the best fit? What are the limitations of working within and across cultures? It seems to me that community outreach work, together with work in primary care settings and the links to a team with experience of such work, all create a context for the flourishing of cross-cultural work.

In exploring these questions, I have found it useful to think in terms of having an insider–outsider position: my insider position derives from my shared personal cultural understanding with the families, while my outsider position derives from our professional

Western training. Often the insider position is in the realm of the unconscious, unexplored, intuitive knowledge of my internal experiences. By my internal experiences I mean the general shared understanding of my culture and the nonverbal or "doxic" aspects of my experiences, which become accessible to me when I am faced with the shared cultural similarities of Bangladeshi families (Bourdieu, 1990). Holding this insider–outsider position is a delicate balance that requires me, as a Bangladeshi therapist, to develop a constantly evolving curiosity. This is negotiated through an internal dialogue in which I keep the insider–outsider position alive. The internal dialogue questions my assumptions coming from my Western training and its fit with the emerging stories told by the families, mediated by my shared cultural understanding.

If we conceptualize engaging with a family as a multilayered process, we then need to be mindful of the fact that we create similarities and differences by the matching of our cultures, languages, and religions. Although it is not useful to homogenize continents, cultures, or families, there is a shared history, similar kinship patterns, and beliefs about health and illness that unites me and the Bangladeshi families with whom I work, making it possible for me to have more access to understanding a family from the same culture and to use a wider range of therapeutic approaches.

CHAPTER EIGHT

A Sure Start rapid-response service for parents and their under fours

Cathy Urwin

This chapter describes a once-weekly rapid-response out-reach clinic for parents and under fours established in a local community centre, initially under the auspices of Sure Start. The model of working was broadly similar to the psychotherapeutically oriented Under Fives Counselling Service developed over many years at the Tavistock Clinic (Miller, 2000). In the chapter I emphasize the combination of local factors that had to be borne in mind in establishing a viable project—one that took as a starting point the needs of the local referral population and the strengths and limitations of our own service. I want to illustrate the potential of this kind of working context for promoting good liaison between statutory and voluntary sectors, reaching hard-to-reach populations, and understanding the impact of cultural difference.

Within child and family mental health services there is a wide recognition that effective services for under fours and their parents must take account of the particular presenting problems and needs

An earlier, longer version of this chapter appeared in the *Journal of Child Psychotherapy 29* (2003): 375–392; published by permission.

of this age group. Most services particularly stress the importance of responding rapidly and offering short waiting times and relatively brief intervals between appointments (see, for example, Barrows, 1999; Miller, 2000; Pozzi, 2003). Responding early can avoid a crisis later on, militating against the considerable strain on young families caused by the typical range of presenting problems, such as sleeping difficulties and unmanageable behaviour. In addition, the very intensity of the impact of infantile experience stirred up by the baby or young child makes this a particularly rich time for promoting learning from experience and developmental change in parents, enabling them to work through some of the unresolved issues from their own childhoods.

These factors apply even more strongly in mental health services for infants, where the cost benefits of early intervention are more or less incontrovertible (Barrows, 2000) and where projects that are tailor-made to the particular needs of the target group are most likely to be successful (Balbernie, 2002). This has been demonstrated particularly clearly in a number of intervention studies in the United States (Shonkoff & Phillips, 2000). In the British context, however, there is a considerable gap between the rhetoric of the importance of early intervention and the development of infant and young child mental health services accessible to the hard-to-reach and, arguably, the sectors of our communities that are most in need. For this reason several child psychotherapists and members of allied professions with an interest in working with this age range have become particularly interested in what can be achieved under the umbrella of Sure Start.

Sure Start is a time-limited, government-funded programme which, since the latter part of the 1990s, has been directed at promoting developmental opportunities and parenting support in certain targeted deprived areas, selected on the bases of demographic factors and deprivation indices. All Sure Start projects involve establishing working partnerships between local community and voluntary sector groups and statutory agencies such as health, mental health, education, and social services. Particular emphasis is placed on consulting parents and involving them in management and decision-making, within projects directed at various government targets. These targets have been subject to review but in general involve improving nutrition and physical health, promoting social, emotional, and linguistic development and cognitive skills, and, for parents, improving employment opportunities and reducing smoking and the impact of postnatal depression.

For child and adolescent mental health services (CAMHS), the most relevant target areas are promoting emotional and social development, militating against the consequences of postnatal depression, and generally supporting the principles of good parenting. In general terms, a CAMHS contribution might seek to offer a range of activities, such as parenting groups, staff supervision and consultation, as well as direct clinical work. To be included in a local Sure Start plan, however, it must be shown that this would be additional to or different from what is available through the mainstream service and must dovetail with the rest of the plan, including the results of the consultation exercise with the local community.

There is considerable diversity in the CAMHS/Sure Start projects established across the country, partly due to varying local factors including ethnic differences and population density, so that there are few general principles for good projects. Furthermore, Sure Start funding is time-limited. It is therefore sensible to design innovations along lines compatible with the direction in which one might wish the mainstream service to develop, since the most likely source of continuing funding is through mainstreaming.

These factors have wider implications for linking statutory and community services. The government green paper *Every Child Matters* (Department for Education and Skills, 2003) and the National Service Framework for Children stress the importance of CAMHS's increasing commitment to working with primary care and community services and developing ways of engaging hard-to-reach groups who would not normally use CAMHS provision, possibly through satellite clinics. However, guidelines on how such work could be established are few, and as yet little is known about the pitfalls and advantages and what would work best in particular areas.

Establishing a need

For several years now, a multidisciplinary under-fives special interest group has regularly carried out surveys of referrals of under fives to the three clinics comprising CAMHS in an inner London borough. Despite a steady increase, some groups have been under-represented. Notably, referrals from certain ethnic groups do not reflect the ethnic breakdown of the community, and babies under 18 months are grossly under-represented. There are also marked effects of geography. A recent local survey of under fives attending two of the clinics revealed that the vast majority of families who kept appointments lived within buggy-pushing distance of the clinics.

That these kinds of factors may discriminate against some of the most disadvantaged families in the borough was thrown into sharp relief with the arrival of Sure Start within the catchment area of one of the three clinics. The Sure Start area, which I will call "Riverside", includes a large GP practice and is centred round the Riverside Estate. Providing temporary accommodation for homeless families, this estate nevertheless houses many families who seldom leave it, although it contains very few leisure facilities. As a whole, the area is characterized by high levels of unemployment and by disturbed and delinquent behaviour in both primary and secondary schools. The largest ethnic group is white British, followed closely by Bangladeshi. Other ethnic and cultural groupings include Caribbean and African, and there are many asylum seekers and refugees from Eastern Europe.

While the primary and secondary schools in the area are good referrers to CAMHS, referrals of under fours have been almost nonexistent. One likely contributing factor is the relatively difficult journey to reach the nearest mainstream clinic. The general argument for early intervention strongly suggests that developing a service accessible to parents of under fours in this area could contribute to reducing the number or severity of difficulties presenting later on.

The rapid-response outreach clinic described here was established as part of a CAMHS–Sure Start project, which also included a commitment to providing consultation, supervision, and group work for Sure Start workers, allied professionals, parents, and others, as required. The outreach clinic itself was to be based in the community and would be run by myself. It would offer relatively brief work, facilitating referral on to the mainstream service or other agencies where appropriate. The nature of the presenting problems and the degree of change would be assessed using the same criteria as in the mainstream service. The parents' assessment of change and service satisfaction would be assessed using a specially designed questionnaire. We would seek to demonstrate an increase in the rate of referrals of under fours from the area receiving our service by comparison with previous rates of referral to the local CAMHS clinic.

After the Sure Start partnership board had agreed to the proposal and welcomed it, we chose to use the funding to release me from my mainstream clinic for one day a week while I established this new service. A new appointee would work exclusively with under fives referred to this clinic, offering a comparable rapid-response, short-waiting-time initiative for the under fours comparable to what I was offering in the Sure Start outreach clinic. A high level of referrals at one of the other two clinics over the same period had meant that under fives had had to be placed on a general waiting list for several months. A waiting-list initiative directed exclusively at families with under fours was established there on a trial basis. Families were contacted by telephone and offered three to five assessment/treatment sessions, to begin within two weeks.

These initiatives within the mainstream service allowed us to make some comparisons between the families attending the Sure Start outreach clinic and families with under fours attending the mainstream service. We looked particularly at presenting problems, referral agencies, ethnicity, waiting times and attendance rates, and family background characteristics. In both the mainstream services, families were to be given a version of the specially designed Sure Start parent satisfaction questionnaire on completion of the work.

In the original plan, the outreach clinic was to be based in the health centre. We thought that, as mothers of babies and toddlers frequently visit the centre for baby clinics and make it a first port of call when they are worried about their older children, it would prove an accessible venue to which parents could refer themselves, or attend at the suggestion of other Sure Start workers as well as GPs and health visitors. In the event, this original plan had to be modified. Though sympathetic to the project, the GPs were, at the last minute, unable to house the project. Instead, the outreach clinic was based in a new community centre. This had always been the first choice of venue for an outreach clinic for many of the members of the Sure Start partnership board. They felt it would be more accessible and less stigmatizing than seeing someone at the GP practice and that, based in a community centre, I would see a broader range of people in genuine need who would not attend a mainstream service. I now believe that they were right.

What's in a name?

The challenge of setting up a new service, in a new organization, within a totally unfamiliar setting, and the learning that has resulted from this, can best be described in terms of a series of shocks. This had begun with finding myself based in the community centre, which had not been my first choice, and continued through the process of writing literature to advertise the project, choosing a name, and into the clinical work itself.

The health visitors had requested a leaflet that they could give to parents when suggesting the service to them, to give them an idea of what kinds of problems could be addressed and what they could expect from attending. I designed a leaflet describing this in a straightforward way, in accessible language, putting it to the partnership board for approval. The leaflet was then evaluated by the parents' consultation group, which sent it back to me, re-written!

On recovering from the blow to my narcissism, I recognized the significance of this communication. First, it was an assertion of the priority to be given to the community as opposed to the health service—an emphasis on "this is what we want" as opposed to a passive acceptance of what I had to offer. Second, the changes that had been made were subtle and important, less to do with content than with style.

My leaflet had given a straightforward description of the kinds of difficulties that infants and young children might present, inviting parents to come for help in addressing them, with some idea about length of treatment and range of interventions, as the health visitors required. The modified version not only advertised what was on offer in a more "punchy" way, but also foregrounded the need to engage parents with the idea that this was a service that would benefit *them*. Thus, the modified version began:

> *How is it going, being a parent? How long since anyone bothered to ask? Are you sick of hearing "It's just a phase they go through?" What if it's not? Who could you ask?*
>
> *This new service is concerned with all the things that concern you as a parent of a baby or a small child.*

Clearly, parents in the parent group knew about postnatal depression and wanted to make sure that I knew of the realities of their lives. They also recognized that getting help with worries about children's development or difficult behaviour from a professional could be a very new idea. These points also had to be borne in mind in naming the service. Nobody wanted such confusing or off-putting words as "clinic" or "health" or "mental" in the title, so we held a competition for the best name, which was won by a parent with the suggestion, "Help at Hand".

The emphasis on a service that was accessible and recognized parents' needs was also built into the questionnaire/feedback form. This asked explicitly about the accessibility of the venue, suitability of the appointment times, and friendliness of the service, as well as whether they had seen improvements in the problems for which they came to the service, in their understanding of the underlying issues and in what they felt about their relationship with their child. The questionnaire was to be given to all parents at their last appointment and was to be filled in before they left the building, on the understanding that their comments would remain anonymous. Questionnaires were to be posted to those families who stopped coming before an agreed final meeting.

The working contract to be offered in each case consisted of an initial consultation, with the offer of up to four further sessions including a review. This could be followed by a further five sessions if necessary, and the possibility of further work or referral on to mainstream services after this. As noted previously, referrals would be taken from parents themselves, Sure Start workers, and professionals in the statutory services serving the community—for example, the nursery schools, the health centre, the local child development team, and other agencies. Accordingly, we developed a referral form, based on a modified version of the one used by the local CAMHS.

A child psychotherapist practises in new terrain

A starting assumption in this project was that it would be possible to take the kinds of skills developed through psychotherapeutic counselling with under fives into the community (Daws, 1985). The distinctiveness of psychotherapeutic work with this age group is the emphasis on the process of thinking about the emotional life of the child and mobilizing the development of fantasy as it reveals itself in the play and interaction within a transference situation. This may apply to the child, to the parent, or to both. It is attention to these processes that informs the therapist about what to ask and when, about the parents' own childhood, for example, in order to facilitate freeing a hitch in the parent–child relationship. The latter often results from the intensity of parents' projections of their own unresolved material onto the child.

In the most benign situations, the "unsticking" is usually associated with the parent seeing the child as a baby or child separate from themselves, with new scope for enjoyment, for finding each other, and for thinking about the problem. Here, I am not averse to asking parents to keep diaries occasionally, or to make observations of the child or of themselves. I also find that some of the principles of Brief Solution Focused Therapy, which emphasizes that clients have the resources within themselves to find solutions to their problems, can be extremely useful in supporting demoralized parents (De Shazer, 1985).

However, the bottom line is that, to function as a psychotherapist, one needs to be able to establish something like a psychotherapeutic setting—a confidential space sufficiently free from intrusion to allow the transference situation to be observed. Agreement was reached at the community centre that each week I would have a particular room, where the work would be private and uninterrupted.

The service opened with its first referral at Easter, initially operating half a day a week; it would then be extended to a whole day a week from the beginning of the autumn term. In the first term I saw eight families, many referred by leaders of playgroups using the community centre. Almost immediately I met a transference issue that I have not met with such intensity when working in a mainstream clinic, since many of the families referred knew each other and might even attend the same group. It occasionally happened that a mother would go back into her playgroup just as her friend was coming out! Inevitably, this heightens competitiveness or intrusiveness, running the risk that one or both mothers drop out.

These kinds of problems are familiar to child psychotherapists working in schools and residential settings, where the therapist's relationships with other patients can become an object of intense curiosity. Here, the situation was helped by finding a room that was more separate from the comings and goings of the centre and by trying to avoid arranging appointment times for two families known to be particularly well acquainted too close together. I found it essential to be absolutely scrupulous about boundary setting and confidentiality. For example, I was careful to restrict to the absolute minimum what feedback I gave to a playgroup leader about a family she had referred. At times I have had to withstand immense curiosity from the centre users. This has meant tolerating being different from other Sure Start workers, but it has been crucial in establishing that the service offers a confidential approach.

The question of feedback to referrers raises another important area where the outreach service is very different from the mainstream service. In the mainstream service, except in the case of self-referrals, it is normally possible and appropriate to give some information back to the referrer. In addition, parents are routinely asked at the first appointment for permission to share information with their GP or health visitor. This permission is seldom refused.

Service users are also asked for consent at the first appointment. Unlike most mainstream service users, it has not been uncommon for the Sure Start families to withhold consent, at least initially.

There are also differences in the manner of referral. In the Sure Start service, self-referrals have remained very uncommon. Despite the availability of a referral form, the more typical approach is for a Sure Start worker to give me a parent's name and telephone number, with a request that I give the parent a telephone call. This works well in many cases, but it raises difficulties when one is concerned about a parent, who then misses subsequent appointments without getting in touch, and there is no obvious agency to inform about the situation. In the case of a referral from a playgroup leader, for example, it would be inappropriate to burden the referrer with sensitive information about a family to which she is not privy. The situation would be particularly sensitive in the case of a parent who said that she did not wish for the GP to be informed of her attendance.

To deal with these kinds of situations, a protocol representing lines of communication and liaison was worked out in supervision, through discussion with Sure Start workers and bearing in mind local child protection procedures. It is subject to constant revision.

Comparison with the mainstream service

The need for a set of procedures over and above what is usually necessary in the mainstream service gives some indication of the nature of the Sure Start referral population. Six months after Help at Hand opened, I had seen 16 families. A comparison between Help at Hand users and the two mainstream clinic samples was possible.

Attendance by families with under fours to the mainstream rapid-response service and to the waiting list initiative was extremely good. It was thought that telephone calls reminding families of appointments had been particularly helpful. Most families attending lived close to their respective clinic. Attendance rates to the first appointment at Help at Hand were high. Thereafter, they were not as good as to the under-fours services in the mainstream clinics, but, at around 60%, they were similar to attendance rates for the service as a whole.

The three user groups did not differ greatly in the range of presenting problems. The most common problem concerned managing difficult behaviour and separation issues, although the mainstream services, appropriately enough, had more complex referrals involving disabilities or illness in the children. All three services saw a broad range of ethnic groups. The representation of Bangladeshi families was surprisingly high, beginning to approximate the proportion in the community. At Help at Hand ethnic groups represented included Bangladeshi, English, Caribbean, Sikh, Irish, Kossovan, and Hispanic.

The most striking differences, discernible when work began rather than necessarily at referral, concerned some of the factors in the backgrounds of the Help at Hand parents. These factors were likely to make it more difficult for them to approach statutory agencies or persons in positions of perceived authority. They included uncertain immigrant status, criminality, and ongoing domestic violence. Other situations where the family attending Help at Hand would have been unable to get to the mainstream service include situations where parents requested confidential consultations, stressing that they did not want other family members to know. One parent, for example, wanted to talk about the implications of a heritable condition in the family for the child's development.

Interestingly, there was one case referred to the mainstream service that was transferred to Help at Hand as it was felt that the Sure Start service would be more likely to engage the parent. This was the mother of a child with a disability. The mother was suspected of having a mental illness. She was no longer responding to telephone calls and could only be contacted by text messaging. This parent attended Help at Hand and made good use of it. Her paranoia or avoidance proved to be associated with some recent traumatic experiences and social problems, which had left her extremely anxious rather than mentally ill.

The first six months of the project, then, suggested that the outreach service was reaching a group of parents who would not otherwise receive our service, that this group was slightly different from our usual service users, and that we had reached them through a slightly different referral route.

The situations in which families were living made the work very anxiety-provoking, but also intensely moving. This was partly to do with the shock of hearing about the high level of loss and deprivation with which most of these families had to deal, a shock that was perhaps intensified by the unfamiliarity of the context in which I was working on the one hand, and of the cultures of the families on the other.

Case study: "Maria"

Maria was referred by the leader of the "under twos club" because she could not stop crying. Her 20-month-old child was becoming increasingly disturbed. It emerged that Maria's father was dying back home in her country of origin. Maria could not leave the country because her immigration status was being queried. Her passport was at the Home Office. She believed that if she retrieved it, she might not be allowed to return to this country. Her British husband said that they could not afford to travel as a family, although they had hoped to do so in the following year.

Maria wept with guilt and anguish at what she imagined of her father's grief at not seeing her and at the fact that she felt trapped in this country, torn in two. In the meantime her little boy, distressed at her tears, nevertheless tried to interest her in the toy plane on the table. It was as if he was trying to say, I can make a plane for you, Mummy, if you will only notice me. I will show you how to fly. Maria was apparently oblivious.

I felt shocked at the inhumanity of a legal process that separated a daughter from her father in this way, with the finality of death in front of them. Recognizing the intensity of Maria's attachment, I felt I could not imagine anything worse. I felt that nothing in my experience approached the awfulness of her situation, particularly the lack of freedom and the powerlessness. I was overwhelmed by the enormity of the gap between our life experiences. Eventually, as Maria told me more of her life and relationship to her father, mother, and siblings, I began to process the countertransference to what I heard, and the internal reality began to percolate. I discovered, after all, the relevance of previous work with fathers and daughters and divided families.

Maria was letting me know about a complex Oedipal situation. Maria had been a bright child in an extremely poor family, carrying much of the ambition for her father. Even now she was expected to send money back home to help pay for his treatment. She nevertheless suffered particularly from the guilt of not being with him, before owning some of her anger at him for not waiting until it was possible for her to visit. She also initially felt severely criticized and blamed by her mother. This severity softened during the course of the work. Through telephone calls she was able to give a lot of support to the rest of the family. She was able to carry out mourning rituals regarded as necessary in her culture in parallel with what was happening back home.

As Maria began to talk more about her feelings and think about her past, the child's behaviour settled, and she was more available to him. She attended eight sessions over a three-month period and returned again a few months later for a review. During this appointment she told me that, when she was a baby, her mother had sold her to an aunt for the equivalent of fifty pence. This is apparently not uncommon in her country, where active displays of attachment and dependence are discouraged and children are expected to help out within the extended family.

Case study: "Ayesha"

In the case of Ayesha, the shock was less to do with my unfamiliarity with her culture of origin than with the nature of what she had to tell me. Ayesha comes from Turkey. She was referred from a women's refuge shortly before the birth of her baby. Her health visitor was concerned about the well-being of mother and baby, and Ayesha wanted someone to talk to. She had told the health visitor that she had another child in her home country with whom her relationship had gone badly wrong. That child was now living with her parents. She was very concerned that things might go wrong with her new baby too.

I met Ayesha when the baby was 12 days old. At the first appointment the baby, "Selena", was asleep. Ayesha told me how, when she was very young, she got involved with a charming but sadistic man who was very unreliable about money. She had run away with him to the city in order to avoid the arranged marriage her parents wanted for her, and had got pregnant. Although she had stayed with them briefly after the baby was born, she returned to the city almost immediately and started working again to support herself and the baby's father. Ayesha wept as she told me that, when her first baby was Selena's age, she would leave him alone in the flat while she went to work, popping back every few hours to feed him in secret.

Ayesha was clearly racked with guilt when she told me this and distressed at how ignorant and thoughtless she felt she had been in those days. At the next appointment, she was more relaxed. It was as if, now that she had unburdened herself of the memory, she had forgotten it. However, she breast-fed Selena throughout most of the session, and through the one after that. She appeared unable to put Selena down. She told me that she got very anxious if the baby cried at night, because she was worried what other people would say about the noise. Perhaps this was reminiscent of her experience with her first baby, making her particularly prone to feeling people would be likely to judge her or assume she would cause the baby harm. She explained that Selena would hold onto the nipple in her mouth long after she had finished feeding, refusing to let go. Why did Selena do that? I asked what she thought. She said, "Is it insecurity?"

Ayesha talked freely about her family and childhood experiences. She also worked over her distress at the end of the relationship with Selena's father, who had felt very excluded by the pregnancy. By my containing and processing the shock of hearing how she had left her first baby alone, remaining nonjudgemental and positive, the work initiated some reduction in the severity of a harsh internal mother, enabling something more nurturing to come to the fore.

A few weeks later Ayesha told me, plainly recognizing an achievement, that she now found that she did not need to be around the other mothers at the refuge all the time, confusing herself with advice from this one and that one. She felt more confident in knowing what was best for Selena. She was gaining support from a community group. She planned to become a student again when Selena was older. She had received a letter from her elder child and, on the telephone, was on better terms with her parents. Selena no longer hung on to the breast. Ayesha showed me how she and Selena had little conversations, mother and baby imitating each other for some time. Ayesha had tape-recorded one of these conversations, to play to Selena when she was older. I felt absolutely clear, as did Ayesha, that she would never abandon this child.

As often happens with families living in the women's refuge, Ayesha was re-housed out of the borough quite suddenly. Unfortunately I lost contact with her. In the letter to the GP, which I hope will be forwarded to her new GP eventually, I commented on the work done but added that I thought that Ayesha might need help again when Selena was 18 months or so, when issues of separation and autonomy were likely to become pressing.

This case is distinctly different from the referrals from the refuge that normally come to the mainstream service. Our usual experience is that these families come once, if at all, but seldom for further appointments. It is possible that the crisis situation that they are in is not conducive to ongoing work. By contrast Ayesha missed few sessions. Perhaps the umbrella of Sure Start, with Help at Hand as something to get involved in alongside a mother–baby group, made it possible for Ayesha to attend.

Case study: "Abdul"

Abdul was a 3-year-old child who had been born prematurely. He had a brother one year younger. He was referred through the school opposite the community centre, where he had failed to settle into the nursery class. He refused to separate from his mother, becoming uncontrollably aggressive, howling and shrieking, then collapsing in tears. His mother was becoming increasingly worried about having to leave the younger brother in order to spend time with Abdul.

I was introduced to Abdul and his mother, neither of whom spoke English, through the playgroup coordinator at a Sure Start fun day. Another Sure Start worker acted as interpreter. The playgroup coordinator explained that she had been the one who had made the home–school liaison visit before Abdul had started school. Abdul and his little brother had been playing at getting in and out of suitcases. I commented that Abdul was a little boy who had come out of his mother very early. An animated conversation between the mother and the interpreter followed, and the mother agreed to come to an appointment the following week. The same Sure Start worker was able to join us as interpreter in this work.

At the first appointment Abdul scowled warily, pressing up against his mother. However, he was wearing his Sure Start cap and carried his school bag containing books and pencils, given out to the new children on the first day of school. I had the strong impression that Abdul wanted to be a "big boy".

In the room, Abdul's mother "Fathima" explained through the interpreter that she thought that, when she left Abdul, he did not believe that she would come back. She gave a vivid account of Abdul's birth, after which he was kept in special care because of low blood sugar. She became pregnant again very quickly, which she had not planned. When Abdul was 6 months old, she had to go into hospital because her blood pressure shot up. She was in and out of hospital for the rest of the pregnancy.

Fathima became very upset in talking about how she had had to leave Abdul at home. She felt very guilty about this. It was especially hard when they had to take him away again at the end of hospital visits. Later, of course, she reappeared at home with a baby. Over the same time period her father had had a heart by-pass operation and had nearly died. He had now returned to Bangladesh.

Abdul spoke no English but nevertheless watched me as well as his mother and provided a kind of running commentary in his play. This indicated his terror of something dangerous inside. He was terrified of the "moo cow" toy, which makes a noise like a cow when turned upside down. Unusually for a small child, he was too frightened to open the Russian dolls to find a smaller one inside. He very deliberately chucked away a cloth brick with a picture of a duck with ducklings on it, and he rummaged in his school bag for a picture in a book showing a series of balloons getting bigger, and bigger, and bigger, before going "pop!"

Abdul's separation difficulties were bound up with his reactions to his mother's pregnancy with his brother and her disappearing when he had probably only just begun to find her after his own birth. The work in this case also involved active liaison with the school. I suggested to the teacher that Abdul was not ready for the school to insist that his mother leave *him*, which was their usual practice, but that Abdul needed help to leave *her*. I took a large football into the school to show how Abdul might be helped to move away from his mother initially, as he would tentatively kick the ball away and go and fetch it. The school put together a basket of toys and learning materials that were special to him—"Abdul's things"—from which he could chose something himself each day. The school worked hard to give Abdul a sense of belonging.

Abdul became more settled in his mother's presence. A talented male teacher was particularly helpful to him. It was noticed that in general Abdul was more at ease and less clinging when his father brought him in. Abdul told his mother that he wanted Daddy to take him to school and Mummy to pick him up. At her request I wrote to the father's college to request that Abdul's father had some time off to help with this settling process, which in the event proved very helpful.

The process was all going very well. I had, however, a problem. Fathima established a very good rapport with the interpreter and talked to her freely. Sometimes I felt isolated and excluded for long periods in our sessions. I thought about the mother's experience, sitting in the school classroom hour after hour, not understanding what was being said, feeling ineffectual in moving the child on, when she had another boy at home who also needed her.

Eventually I asked, "What happens in Bangladesh? How do parents help their children separate?" Fathima immediately became animated. For a start, in Bangladesh children do not go to school until they are 6 years old, and by that time they are ready. Small children are put in the charge of older children, or they go out on their own to watch the men. At 4 years old many children will wash their own clothes! They may only have two sets, and they wash them when they wash their bodies and spread them in the sun to dry. It is important to change clothes often because of the heat. Also at four, children will go to the shop! This would, of course be a simple stall selling a small choice of vegetables, in view of the house.

As we could then explore, the strong sense of community support and relative freedom in rural Bangladesh is very different from the experience of bringing up children in a high-rise flat, with all the dangers of an urban environment. Fathima's answers are particularly interesting because it is often assumed that, because Bangladeshi parents emphasize the importance of family ties and obligations so strongly, there are no well-established ways in which they aid their children's autonomy.

Fathima plainly valued these questions. The following week the appointment had to be cancelled because the interpreter could not attend the appointment. I asked her to let Fathima know that I would observe Abdul at school instead. Later that day the interpreter rang me. Fathima had rung her and asked her to let me know that Abdul had told her that "The lady from my [sic] centre came to see me at school." This communication, and the mother's wish to share it, indicates the considerable connecting and learning that had been going on.

Abdul's mother enrolled in a parent–toddler group; she did not want Abdul's brother to have similar difficulties. She plans to take English classes. A further consequence of the work was expressed at the school. On the basis of this intervention, I was asked if I could provide some inset training on settling children into nursery. Together with Sure Start colleagues, we organized an event in which my contribution was to foreground the importance of attachment to and separating from parents as an emotional process.

One of the benefits of the day was that it brought "the baby" into the classroom. The value of this has been elaborated particularly clearly by Gladstone and Slack (2003) in describing what they have gained, as teachers and trainers in Early Years Education, by working with mental health professionals through Sure Start. At our event, the staff commented on coming to recognize how important they are to the children as attachment figures. Another development was the idea that, for Bangladeshi parents, the school itself has to take on some of the functions of the supportive community back home.

Conclusion

In a recent paper describing psychoanalytically informed work with two Bangladeshi young women, a mother and an adolescent, Loshak highlights a problem experienced by many helping professionals working across cultures. "Confronted with family patterns so distant from their own experience, and without a shared language, [they] can become overwhelmed and paralysed in their thinking and in their capacity to be of use" (Loshak, 2003, p. 53). Loshak refers to "an unconscious assumption that cultural difference cannot be understood" and that therefore the work will be of limited value. This can lead to stereotypical responses, like the notion of a "culture clash", resulting in a dismissive attitude to the work, or a failure to engage with the grave seriousness of patients' situations and emotional disturbance. She stresses the importance of working with and through the countertransference in these situations.

   In this chapter I have attempted to illustrate the subjective experience of coming up against cultural difference through referring to a series of "shocks". The project I have described has been successful in bringing in and treating under fours and their parents who would not otherwise have attended a CAMHS provision—a

result achieved through moving out into a new working environment. The experience of difference has included the impact of
working with the voluntary sector and of being based in a community centre, in the absence of the protection of usual communication systems, as well as the more obvious one of working with
families from very different cultural backgrounds from my own.

This work has been extremely moving, and also challenging
and anxiety-provoking. Working with a high-risk population, I
often found that I had to establish a network, with clearly defined
gate-keeping procedures and lines of communication, as I went
along. During the initial phase of establishing the service, I particularly valued discussions with colleagues in the mainstream service.
The latter functioned something like a "brick mother" in providing
a solid bedrock of experience; I do not think it is possible to do
outreach work without this kind of secure base. Opportunities for
consultation and supervision are essential.

Negotiating premises, referral procedures, and liaison networks are a necessary part of establishing a viable context for
psychotherapeutic intervention. In this brief work I have seen
myself less as aiming to "cure" children's problems than as giving
the parents and children a good experience, which might at the
very least provide a model for getting professional help later on if
necessary. Clearly, child mental health professionals from many
disciplines would have a great deal to bring to this kind of project.
As a child psychotherapist, what I feel I have been particularly able
to offer is a capacity to think rather than react when under pressure
of anxiety. This is itself fostered through the experience of infant
observation and the development of observation skills. Infant observation is the bedrock of the child psychotherapy training, but it
is increasingly available as an adjunct to the training of many
mental health professionals. I have also found it valuable to have a
well-rounded view of development across the life span.

By the end of the second six months, a year after Help at Hand
had opened, I had worked with 25 families. The main identifying
features of the referral population had been maintained. By now
there was a broader spread of referral agencies, including Sure
Start speech therapists and other professionals. There were also
more referrals from GPs and from nursery schools, suggesting that
the project was taking hold within the statutory sector too. The

proportion of Bangladeshi families attending the service now re-flected the proportion in the community. Attendance rates have improved as I have made more use of telephone calls to remind parents about appointments. The number of questionnaires re-turned to date has been slightly higher than in the mainstream service. These questionnaires have been very positive.

At the end of the first year we learned that Riverside Sure Start could not continue to fund Help at Hand beyond a further six months because of financial pressures within the project as a whole. At the same time we learned that, as an extremely deprived area, CAMHS in the borough would receive extra funding, to be spent in line with the directives put forward in the National Service Framework for children's mental health services. The popularity of Help at Hand has meant that many local organizations and indi-viduals are keen to see it continue. Its success in reaching disadvan-taged groups has meant that it will be included in a planned expansion of under-fives service provision. Though funded by the National Health Service, it will be managed through a working partnership between CAMHS, the local health centre, the commu-nity centre and its users group, the school opposite, with a member of the Sure Start partnership board as a representative. Time will tell whether this project can continue to be productive.

CHAPTER NINE

Making meaning out of the mess: developing the mental health role of health visitors

Ann Simpson

Health visitors and general practitioners are usually the first port of call for parents who are worried about their child's health. However, child mental health problems cannot be solved within the duration of an appointment that a busy GP can offer, while referral to a specialist child mental health service may be more than a parent wants, the child needs, or those services can adequately respond to. Some 80% of children with mental health problems do not reach the specialist services, and neither of the primary nor secondary services presently responds comprehensively to the needs of young children and their parents.

In this chapter I describe a collaborative project that was set up between health visitors, GPs, and a local child and family consultation service, in order to provide early intervention for children under five and their parents where there were emotional and behavioural difficulties. Money was provided for one year for the project, which was also intended to develop the mental health role of health visitors in the local community. The aims of the project were:

- to identify the existing skills and competencies of health visitors working with the mental health needs of preschool children and their families;

- to assess the training, development, and supervision of health visitors in relation to the assessment and treatment of basic mental health problems in preschool children;

- to design and provide training opportunities to meet the identified needs;

- to train and develop two health visitors as course organizers and trainers as a local resource for primary care colleagues;

- to assess the benefits of developing health visitors in this role and the subsequent effects on accessibility and quality of care to children and their families;

- to assess the benefits of this approach to care both within primary care and within the specialist children's mental health services.

Reasons for setting up the project

Early identification of vulnerable families and the implementation of intervention strategies can help to promote positive mental health and change patterns of behaviour. This can result in breaking the cycle of disadvantage. Early intervention work can in some cases break cycles of deprivation and provide positive mental health improvements for children and their families. The current shortfall in the provision of such work seems largely due to a lack of training in assessment and treatment, of specialist supervision and in particular a failure to develop the mental health role of health visitors who could be key practitioners in identifying the need for early intervention.

The government report *Child and Adolescent Mental Health Services: Together We Stand* (Department of Health, 1995) suggests that parents should first seek help from primary care and that only a minority of children with severe or intractable disorders should be referred on to the specialist child and adolescent mental health services. It also suggests that training for this work will be necessary for primary care. The *National Service Framework for Mental*

Health (Department of Health, 1999) identifies the need for health improvement programmes for healthy schools and healthy neighbourhoods, emphasizing the importance of identifying individuals and families in distress. It proposes that service users should have their mental health needs identified and assessed in primary care and supports the idea of specialist mental health services providing primary care liaison and support for primary care staff through continuing professional development.

The National Service Framework for Children promotes partnership working within services including those for children and families whose needs are complex and persistent (Department of Health, 2004). It requires these services to be coordinated and integrated across health, education, social care, youth justice, and voluntary sector agencies. It also requires services to be organized around the child. It recognizes that specific skills are needed for the consultation and liaison work involved in partnership work, and it advocates joint training for effective collaborative working.

A number of parenting programmes have developed over recent years to address the help needed for children and families. Health visitors have been actively recruited and involved in these training programmes. The main models of these parenting groups are the Caroline Webster-Stratton Incredible Years Parenting Programme, Systemic Training for Effective Parenting (STEP), and Parents in Partnership, the Parent Infant Network (PIPPIN), as well as more local initiatives in communities, social services, family centres, and the excellent work of Home Start in the voluntary sector with the under fives. These models, although diverse, do seem to have common shared aims: to increase a parent's self-esteem, to set clear limits, to recognize children as individuals, to empower them to make their own choices wherever possible, and to impart how to use non-violent discipline. They are usually time-limited programmes of about ten to twelve weeks.

While these models are important, none of them addresses in an exploratory way the emotional world of the child and parent and the impact this can have upon the worker. Nor do they promote the idea of professionals working with this therapeutically, in order to deepen their understanding of human relationships and to develop skills and capacities to explore with families issues around mental and emotional ill health that can evoke strong feelings such as fear, anxiety, anger, impotence, confusion, frustration, blame, and a sense of despair and failure. Indeed, health visitors themselves often refer to this kind of approach as opening "a can of worms", and it is understandable if they do not wish to open it without anyone to provide support and backup. It is here that specialist clinical supervision and training holds the key to how much one allows oneself to become involved with behaviour and emotional difficulties in children and families.

The project

As the senior nurse within the local child and adolescent mental health service, I was appointed project lead and clinical supervisor. I had for some time been running work discussion seminars for local health visitors and offering joint assessment work with re-ferred families where children were under five. I was involved from the outset with the locality manager in deciding to advertise for two health visitors to begin the project. The selection panel comprised myself as the project leader, the locality manager, and a senior local general practitioner. Essential and desirable criteria were drawn up, indicating what we were looking for two regis-tered health visitors with a particular interest in the mental health of preschool children and their families and in the aims and objec-tives of the project. They should have at least two years' post-registration experience and be able to demonstrate a keen interest in developing skills relating to the emotional impact of family relationship systems and dynamics on child mental health. They would also need to be interested in the emotional world of the child and family and in the importance of exploring this as means of assessing appropriate intervention. The health visitors would need to be open to thinking and reflecting on their experiences with families and professional networks as a way of informing and developing clinical practice. They should have a clear sense of their own professional role, have presentation and training skills, and be able to offer consultation to other professionals and voluntary groups.

Two health visitors were duly selected. They brought with them considerable health visitor experience and a great interest in mental health, demonstrated already by attending courses with a focus on using psychotherapeutic skills with children and parents.

To begin with, the project leader and health visitors jointly drew up protocols. The health visitors would work one day per week on the project, giving them time to assess families and carry out home interventions for half of the day. The second half would be used for clinical supervision and theoretical reading connected to the clinical work, this being done with the project leader. (Reading clinical papers allowed us to connect theory with practice.) Each health visitor would accept referrals from two GP practices and the health visitors connected to these practices.

A flyer was designed for professionals and families, and the health visitors visited and spoke with the GPs and other health visitors involved. The project health visitors described the ideas behind it and explained that they would be looking for referrals of families whose own GPs and health visitors felt that they were posing difficulties by not responding sufficiently to the intervention of the GP, and also of families who, the GP and practice health visitor thought, might benefit from the outset from a referral to the project.

This preparatory work highlighted:

- the importance of the GP and the practice health visitor discussing the family together before a referral was made to the project;
- the importance of the GP and the practice health visitor preparing the family for such a referral;
- the anxieties that were aroused by families whom the GP and health visitor wanted to refer on.

This beginning process took time and investment, to ensure that the project had the best possible start and that the GPs and practice health visitors were sufficiently included. This process of communication with the GP and health visitors remained ongoing throughout the project. When referrals seemed to dry up, communication and discussion was started again; half-way through the project one of the project health visitors cast a wider net and involved another GP practice and health visitor, requiring a further meeting and discussion of the project with them. Continuous discussion with these referrers prior to and during the work of the families referred was crucial to the development of the project and the intervention made with the families.

Over time it became clear that, on the surface, many children appeared to have emotional and behavioural problems that might be helped by short intervention work, but in fact this did not really prove to be the case. The evaluation of cases referred told us, rather, that the problems identified by the health visitors at assessment were often more complex than they initially appeared. We began to realize that we were having to think about the emotional behavioural struggles of the parents as much those of the children. In the event, only one family referred required short intervention particularly targeted at the child's behaviour, and the parents were quickly able to change this after discussion with the health visitor. Other families turned out to require ongoing involvement in order to examine the relationship between parents and child, particularly mother and child—although three cases involved some in-depth work with the fathers too.

The health visitors and I came to realize that the difficult emotional and behavioural problems of some children can be addressed quickly by parents who have sufficient emotional capacities and ego strength to adopt a firm and thoughtful approach to their children—particularly if they are in a relationship of strength with each other that allows the children's needs to take priority. However, with the majority of families referred to this project— and, indeed, possibly with a large proportion of families on some health visitors' caseloads—the parents, particularly the mothers, are extremely vulnerable themselves. In that situation it is much more of a struggle to find a balance between the children's needs and parental needs.

I would now like to describe two cases of children that were referred to the project.

Case study: "Darren"

The 4-year-old boy of a single mother aged 19 had been excluded from nursery because of his disruptive and aggressive behaviour. Darren's extended family thought him to be a bit of a bad lot. One family member had served a prison sentence for grievous bodily harm, and adolescent boys in the family were thought to be heading in the same direction. The project health visitor recognized the dangers in that this small boy was already becoming socially excluded, gaining a label, and perhaps heading for trouble when he started infant school. Exploration of the mother's early experience and the emotional effect on her of her son's behaviour went some way to settling down an anxious situation, the mother being able to regain more of a position of control over her son, her confidence having been diminished in the face of critical parents, who were also important to her.

This young mother had made some real emotional contact with the health visitor, who helped her to get in touch with her son's father, who, in turn, began to become a supportive figure to them both. This contact also included his parents, the little boy's grandparents. This all took shape within six meetings, and the health visitor was able to involve the nursery nurse to help mother and son with play. That began to restore and repair the relationship, so that the mother was able to recognize the importance of more consistent involvement on her own part and that of more helpful extended family members in order to change a difficult situation.

Darren will probably need some continual monitoring, but this raises the issue of what happens when he gets into the school system and perhaps makes professionals anxious again. We know from this assessment that this vulnerable mother responded very well to the relevant psychological support offered, but it has to be anticipated that the child might get himself excluded again when he is in school. Will anyone think to contact the health visitor, who at this point in time holds relevant information about what interventions the family can respond to best, as well as the difficult family history that might inform other professionals?

This leaves us with a question about the role of the health visitor in cases like this, where further trouble may be anticipated. This case highlights what a good idea it would be for the health visitor, along with the GP, to remain as community consultants to this family—but, of course, in reality she will hand him over to the school system.

Case study: "Mrs Brown"

The mother in this case is an example of someone who would not at this time have been able to have made use of a parenting programme.

Mrs Brown, a 36-year-old married woman with three children under five years of age, attempted suicide twice in the space of two weeks—the first time by overdose, the second by cutting herself. She was admitted to a psychiatric ward on the second occasion but not the first and was allowed discharge within 48 hours. Mrs Brown had a history of postnatal depression after the birth of her second child, "Jay", now aged 3½. Her other children are "Katie", aged 4½, and "David", 6 months.

The health visitor was contacted by the mental health social worker who advised her on the recent chain of events. The GP also voiced his concerns to her and sent off two referrals, one to the psychotherapy services and the other to the cognitive behavioural service.

The health visitor brought this situation to me to explore in supervision, thinking in particular of the needs of the children. Initially she was concerned that Mrs Brown's problems were beyond the scope of her experience and expertise, and she really did not want to become involved. She felt that if she met with Mrs Brown, she might be opening up a can of worms and putting herself in a position of not being able to deal with what she might unearth. She was not sure of the severity of Mrs Brown's mental health problems, and she was concerned that she herself might be too fragile or vulnerable to tolerate what she viewed as her inexperience in this situation.

As supervisor, I explored these very valid feelings with her, which then allowed her to begin to think about how she might be allowing her own vulnerabilities to interfere with her involvement. The health visitor was worried that she might find some emotions too disturbing or painful, and she also wondered whether she might lose control of the situation. She was beginning to think about possibly starting to work in a new way, but at the same time she was frightened and anxious. Discussing these anxieties made a difference, so that she was able to make contact with Mrs Brown. She was also able to withstand the impact on her of several visits to the family.

On her visits, the health visitor noted that the children, although well cared for physically, were anxious, with the middle child protesting most about things and the baby almost always alarmingly quiet, while both Mr and Mrs Brown were completely out of touch with any difficulties the children might be experiencing regarding their mother's absence and distress. Her husband, although frightened by this situation, coped by distancing himself and by staying even longer at work—a situation that fuelled his wife's wish to hurt him in some way.

The health visitor felt distressed, angry, and useless as a consequence of Mrs Brown's wish to deny her difficulties. Mrs Brown went shopping, had tanning sessions, and spent much time at the gym, leaving the children in the care of others, including a new nanny, who was employed to rescue a deteriorating situation (and no doubt to avoid the anxiety and pain of facing up to her disturbance and its impact upon the family). On one occasion when the health visitor visited, the two girls had wandered away from home and had to be brought back by the police. While the health visitor tried to explore how frightening this must have been for them all, Mrs Brown wanted to make light of it and insisted that the girls had been on a big adventure.

The health visitor came away from that visit feeling physically sick and utterly hopeless and useless as she got into her car. Supervision helped her to think about and understand why these feelings were being evoked in her and why she felt she was getting it all wrong and saw no useful reason to keep on going. (She felt she was "banging her head against a brick wall".) It was therefore important to untangle and separate out what belonged to the health visitor and what did not. The health visitor had been trying her best to alert Mrs Brown to a potentially dangerous situation that could not be faced, so she ended up carrying all of this fear, anxiety, and hopelessness that was projected into her. Mrs Brown wanted to rid herself of any feeling about this and so lodged them in the health visitor, who experienced wanting to cut herself off from the situation in just the way Mrs Brown did. The "brick wall" was in fact the defence used by Mrs Brown to prevent anyone breaking through to the mess inside, which was far too frightening to know about.

This situation was nothing to do with an inept health visitor. However, one can begin to see how overwhelmingly pressured the health visitor felt to give up and withdraw. This might have happened without a space to think, to understand, and there-fore to develop with the help of a specialist supervisor. This was all an enormous relief to the health visitor. She was thus able to keep going.

Something was given up at this time by Mrs Brown, who decided to leave her husband and apply for council accommo-dation for herself and the children. She went to live with her mother, uprooting the children from their homes and nurseries. However, there was, for the first time, a glimmer of hope in that she telephoned the health visitor to let her know what she was doing, and wondered if the health visitor would like the ad-dress of her mother. This was the first real indication that she felt a need to be in touch. Supervision helped us to see this moment as a significant change, and the health visitor wrote a letter to her while she was away as a way of maintaining the connection. It may have been this that then helped Mrs Brown ring the health visitor on her return and ask her to visit.

At that visit, which was in the new council house, Mrs Brown conveyed again a sense that she was happy with her new situation. The health visitor felt this to be a cover-up—perhaps like the new decorations—and this time found a way of saying so, at which point Mrs Brown broke down in tears, saying that she felt it was all too much being on her own with the children.

This whole process took eight months. Mrs Brown did not take up any of the therapies she was offered, and she wrote an amorous letter to her GP, who took her off his list. So the health visitor is left holding these babies along with the social worker, and the work goes on.

This case gives a glimpse into a model of how to develop psychological capacities in the health visitor. The model is one that gives meaning to the mess experienced both by the patient and by the health visitor herself and shows how the emotional world of the health visitor can be used to inform clinical practice. It demonstrates how the feelings generated by mental and emotional ill health are communicated to nurses by patients and families, and how the professional can use these responses to therapeutic effect. Professionals working with such cases need to be in touch with why they feel the way they do. This can then be constantly worked through in order to keep them going—but only by developing and learning new skills and by gaining confidence. This probably means consistent specialist supervision—and I want to emphasize the *consistent*.

Conclusion

The project has allowed the space and time to examine individual and family dynamics in some depth and has allowed the health visitors involved to take more risks in exploring thoughts and feelings with a child and family. This can make changes in allowing families to be more emotionally in touch with each other. There would seem to be an element of "hidden illness", particularly in parents, that can seem to have quite a devastating effect on their children. Crucially, this is where child and adolescent mental health services and adult mental health services have to work more closely together.

I would highlight the lessons of the project as these:

1. the increasing mental health role of the health visitor;

2. the potential for developing the role of health visitors in working at the interface of primary care and secondary specialist services for both children and adults;

3. the need to develop the skills of health visitors so that they can explore the emotional impact on themselves of vulnerable children and families, and use their understanding of this as a clinical tool for exploring distressing situations that disable family functioning;

4. the way that psychotherapeutic concepts such as transference and countertransference, holding and containment can be used to influence both clinical practice and consultation with other professionals in the primary and secondary networks;

5. the importance of developing health visitors' skills and competence in the assessment of the mental health needs of children and adults so that they know what intervention they can make themselves and when a referral onto a specialist service is necessary.

6. the continuous need to liaise and communicate with other professionals so that patients do not fall between gaps—inevitably the dynamics of some families influence and split professionals, and this should constantly be taken into account: if communicating with other professionals is proving difficult, this is an issue that must always be asked and thought about.

7. the need of health visitors for a safe place to explore such issues in this way—and therefore the need for consistent clinical supervision.

In conclusion, what child mental health professionals need most of all is a safe place to discuss the impact of the work upon them—a place where transference and countertransference, holding and containment, and the professionals' feeling responses to children and families and situations can all be used as clinical tools to understand and explore the relational dynamics that would otherwise not be tackled, often to the detriment of freeing things up more for the families and putting parents more in emotional touch with the children they experience as difficult. The further development of working in this way could lead on to higher levels of practice by health visitors. It would be heartening to see the day when a health visitor is an integral part of all local CAMHS teams, perhaps having a bridging role between that team and the primary network.

CHAPTER TEN

The practice as patient: working as a psychotherapist in general practice

Jo O'Reilly

This chapter explores the relationship between primary care and psychotherapy from the perspective of a psychotherapist working in a GP surgery. Psychotherapeutic and primary care models apply different approaches to our patients, and the presence of a psychotherapist in the practice has an impact on the practice as a whole. The interface at which the two meet can represent a highly sensitive but potentially fertile ground and an opportunity to explore what it is that our patients are requesting of us. It can, however, also present particular difficulties—for example, if the practice feels threatened or persecuted by the therapist's approach. There are also anxieties for the therapist who works inside another institution, especially one as potentially cohesive as a general practice. The placement of a therapist within a practice may be one way to build stronger links with our referrers, but it requires careful consideration as there is a risk of confusion as to the aims and identity of the work.

An earlier version of this chapter appeared in *Psychoanalytic Psychotherapy*, *14* (2000): 253–266.

In this chapter I describe the development of my relationship as a psychotherapist with a GP surgery. I visited the practice on a weekly basis over a two-year period. Patients referred by the practice were seen and discussed with the practice staff at regular monthly meetings. I learned how the position I occupied in the mind of the practice, together with my own thoughts about my role, were key factors influencing both the possibilities and limitations of the work. Many of us have a transference to GPs of some awe and deference; as a doctor myself, I am less vulnerable to this, but perhaps an element remained. I therefore paid particular attention to how the GPs regarded my work, as evidenced by their referrals and other contacts with me. I also experienced a shift in my own thinking about the work, from an initial model of assessing the referred patients for psychotherapy to more of a "third position" of experiencing and thinking about the patients within the practice. This involved the need to identify with the GPs while preserving the space to think.

A GP surgery is an environment of intense anxiety and intimacy, and so for a psychotherapist there are complex boundary issues to negotiate. This also means there is a wealth of material available about the anxieties and fantasies of the practice staff about the therapist. I therefore discuss the question of how to engage most usefully with the GPs as something crucial to the work, worthy of the same thought and concern as the referred patients. The idea of the "practice as a patient" is introduced as a helpful model in thinking about the work, borrowing from pre-existing ideas of psychoanalytic consultancy work within which the institutional dynamics of an organization may be considered in the same way as a patient. There is also the paradox that, in the company of GPs on their own ground, any of us may feel like patients ourselves. The complexities of these dynamics are illustrated with material from meetings with the GPs and the work with patients.

The beginning

The Adult Department at the Tavistock has a long history of staff placements in GP practices. The practice described here had expressed an interest in having a psychotherapist working there on a sessional basis and had presented as seeming to be keen and interested, but with a background of dissatisfaction with the department, since they felt that their patients were never taken on for treatment. From the outset I felt a pressure to repair a negative view of the department and was interested to what extent this would be possible and was realistic.

The practice occupies an old building that had been extensively modernized, giving a sense of space and light. There is an open-plan reception area with easy access to patients' notes. The GPs collect patients in person for the appointments, and staff and patients are in this way exposed to each other—a situation that is quite different from the more protected contact that takes place within a psychotherapy department. This meant that I regularly met both GPs and patients who may or may not have had appointments with me that morning, in the reception area. This access to me, often taking the form of an attempt by the patients to establish or avoid a contact, or of an unguarded comment or conversation with a GP, presented rich material about both the patient's and the practice's state of mind in relation to the presence of a therapist in the practice.

At the time of my attachment, the practice comprised four partners and two practice nurses who also attended the meetings between myself and the GPs. The increased exposure and intimacy on an informal basis between the referrers, the patients, the practice staff and me presented issues about personal and professional boundaries, often in a very swift way, that I needed to consider. From the outset my presence seemed to arouse considerable anxiety and curiosity, sometimes most directly expressed by the non-medical staff. While they were always helpful and friendly, I also felt there was wariness and uncertainty about how to relate to me, with jokes among the reception staff about their own need to be referred and a wish to let me know more straightforwardly something of their own lives and difficulties. The friendliness of the reception staff can in fact be a major factor in helping an outside professional manage within an institution.

On starting in the practice, I was struck by a feeling of capacity and was given a choice of rooms. One of these was an unused GP room and the other a room referred to as the "counselling-room", which is the one I chose. This was upstairs in the practice and separate from the GPs' consulting-rooms. The practice seemed aware of my needs and provided a small table and comfortable chairs. Interruptions were few. A computer in the room, linked to reception, indicated when my patients had arrived. As winter approached, I became aware that the heating in the room was broken, and there also developed an unpleasant smell of rotting drains. When I raised this, a heater was found and a drain company called, but with some embarrassment among the practice staff. There was a sense of the practice being aware that they had presented some kind of a communication to me. When raised in the GP meetings, there was embarrassment and something of an over-compensation. I subsequently arrived to do my work to find two fires on in an overheated room.

Initial meeting with the GPs

The first meeting with the GPs was characterized by a friendliness and certain briskness towards me. Practical issues were addressed and easily agreed upon. The GPs readily agreed about the importance of regular meetings and had in mind a suitable monthly slot. They were clearly preoccupied about whom to refer to me, and this was linked to their statement that they had stopped referring patients to the psychotherapy department, as they did not get taken on for treatment. (Interestingly, their impressions and beliefs about the lengths of waiting lists and likelihood of patients being taken on for treatment were considerably more pessimistic than the reality of the treatment options and waiting lists in the department.) There was, however, quite a hopeful feeling that this was something they wanted help with, rather than taking a more ag-grieved position in relation to it. This help seemed to be in the form of guidelines or diagnostic categories of patients I would be interested in seeing.

My suggestion that meetings could provide an opportunity to think about referrals and why they may wish me to see a particular patient was followed by a hasty request for some recommended reading on the subject. I felt I was related to as representing part of the department, temporarily located in the GP surgery, with not much opportunity to think about how a therapist might link with them as a team. No requests were made of me in this meeting, and the practice staff seemed to have, on the one hand, a readiness to fit in and, on the other, a feeling of needing help, represented by their preoccupation of what comprised an "appropriate" referral. There was some relief when I described the work as a collaborative process from which both parties could learn.

GP meetings

I met monthly with the GPs and the practice nurses. The meetings were always well attended, although in the early months lateness was typical. From the outset I felt acutely aware of the impact my presence had on the practice staff, and of the myriad ways this could be expressed. Characteristic was the manner of the GPs arriving at the meetings: rushed and with a pile of messages and an urgent need to discuss medical matters in a manner that excluded me. Meetings were always lively and full, and there was typically a pressure to feel rushed and to discuss patients briefly in a "management meeting" style. It was as if there was a wish to let me know of the pressures they were under, but in a way that meant it never quite was expressed or attended to.

In one of the early meetings one of the doctors arrived in a very harassed state, announcing that "we must decide what we are going to do about Viagra". It did, indeed, seem that the doctors wanted me to know of both their potency and their helplessness in face of the demands their patients made of them. A fragile tension between a view of themselves as omnipotent and without needs themselves and a much more collapsed and helpless view of their abilities to meet their patients' needs was to be a recurring theme in their contact with me. The GPs' propensity to feel persecuted and their difficulty of seeing when they had done something well were also striking—as if there was a fear that I would be terribly critical of them.

With time, my presence seemed less persecutory to the practice staff, and as my anxiety and theirs lessened, the ability to think and reflect grew. There was less lateness and a clearer sense of the meetings as representing something different from a medical meeting yet valued in its own right. It seemed as if referrals to me peaked at times the practice was stressed, such as when I first started and before Christmas. It was possible to raise this with them as an indication of the pressures they were under, which could be acknowledged without making the GPs feel criticized or ashamed.

It also became increasingly possible for the meetings to have a more thoughtful feel in discussing patients. This seemed to have developed alongside the recognition and understanding of psycho-therapy as a long-term treatment that usually does take time if enduring change is to occur, which initially seemed puzzling to the GPs. Often they had all had contact with the patient or with members of the patient's family, and this was discussed; it was apparent that they were not familiar with the process of thinking about or discussing their patients' lives in a coherent sense with each other and that it was quite a relief and source of pleasure for them to do so. Additionally, the unique knowledge the practice had of many of the patients and their extended families added a richness of clinical material to be thought about psychodynami-cally.

The opportunity for both myself and the GPs to say something about our experience of individual patients and how their presen-tation could be understood in terms of their earlier development and life experiences felt invaluable. The GPs were quick to learn something of the transference and countertransference and of what important figures they might represent transferentially to their patients. Recognition that their emotional responses to their pa-tients were worthy of careful consideration in capturing something of the patients' difficulties seemed to afford quite a relief to the GPs, and they showed considerable interest in thinking in this way. This seemed helpful in developing a less beleaguered attitude towards some of their most demanding patients.

There grew an increasing recognition that patients were often referred because of some difficulty in the relationship between GP and patient. One of the partners who was trained in cognitive behavioural therapy (CBT) told me: "I see patients for CBT and refer them to you when I feel a transference interpretation needs to be made." I came to see one aspect of my role as both a container of the GPs' anxieties and as facilitating their own capacities to metabolize and understand something of their patients' difficulties. Alongside their acknowledged disappointment that I was not able to take on or take away some of their most troubling patients was the recognition that as their patients' GPs, they usually represented the most enduring and important relationship the patient had with health services.

In the primary care setting, there is a unique opportunity for close contact between the therapist and the GP, which can be crucial in allowing anxiety and projections generated by patients to be contained and splitting to be seen and understood. This process can be vital in treating patients psychotherapeutically for whom treatment has previously proved impossible, as illustrated by a patient I shall refer to as Sally.

Case study: "Sally"

Sally was a 40-year-old woman with a 9-year-old son, "Kim", and a history of extreme childhood deprivation and abuse. In her experience, good objects left while perverse and cruel objects were both familiar and survivable. Extreme splitting involving multiple agencies and escalating anxiety had characterized her previous treatments, and attempts at psychotherapy in the past had quickly broken down. After an initial assessment, I saw her for regular fortnightly sessions for 24 months, and through this work and regular discussions with the GPs, containment and some treatment were possible.

A hallmark of the treatment was the ever-present anxiety in someone's mind—be it myself, the GP or one of the practice staff—that psychotherapy and its powerful effect on her was making her worse. This reached a peak when she accused her neighbour of sexually abusing her son, with whom she had an extremely enmeshed relationship. Through close contact with the surgery, these crises could be understood in terms of her complex, perverse, and at times psychotic transference to me. As she brought more of her disturbance to her sessions, her GP noticed some improvement in her relationship with him, in her ability to recognize and articulate her own feelings and to make more appropriate use of the surgery as a helpful object. As she developed some separation internally from her son, the practice were able to let me know that he became less anxious and that his mother developed an increasing ability to recognize his needs and difficulties, for the first time making separate appointments for him with a doctor different from her own. Sally's ability to generate anxiety was considerable, and the opportunity to contain and try to understand what she was presenting to a number of different professionals in the GP meetings was probably essential to the survival of her treatment. Interestingly, once I left the practice and ended this work, the patient was for the first time able to make the transition to a long-term once-weekly treatment in the psychotherapy department.

Boundary issues

Within the quickness and liveliness of the meetings with the practice staff, I became aware at times of a risk of the discussion suddenly degenerating into something more informal and gossipy, which could feel denigratory to my work and patients. At these times I felt a pressure to join a complicated feeling of comfortableness with the GPs in which they were keen to make me join with them as one of a beleaguered team, together in their exasperation with patients. I am myself medically trained, and it seemed pleasing to the GPs that I, too, was a doctor and in this sense was like them. Evidence of my differences from them would, however, seem to increase their anxiety. The practice nurse would bring sandwiches for herself and the doctors to the meeting, and the fact that I did not have one would be commented on with an expression of uncertainty and regret. It felt as if this external statement of difference represented something of an important internal boundary it was necessary to maintain against the pressure to be the same as them. From their perspective I may have seemed to be maintaining this boundary too strictly—and perhaps in retrospect a bit of blurring might have been a relief to everyone. The GPs' intense interest in me would also be indirectly expressed by their slipping in quick questions about my training, psychoanalysis, and the psychotherapy department, and on one occasion expressing a wish for a session with a patient to be videoed so that they could all see it.

Part of the anxiety that a therapist's presence generated in the GPs seemed to be a belief that I could see right into them and know all about them. It seemed that in their preoccupation with making what I would consider "suitable" referrals they were seeking reassurance that it was the patients they were referring, not unconscious aspects of themselves. Both were probably true to varying extents, and as the GPs began thinking more about why they were referring particular patients, I needed a clear view of my task and an understanding of countertransference to help them to negotiate the boundary between the personal and the unconscious communication from the patient. I learned to recognize moments of uncertainty or lack of clarity in a GP's discussion of a patient as sometimes being evidence of a projective process between patient and doctor, or doctor and therapist. At these times it seemed that the robustness of the internal model of psychoanalytic work was of paramount importance in maintaining a separate reflective, clear position in order to support the GPs in their roles as the patients' doctors. There were also occasions when I was aware of the GPs discussing patients using expressions I myself might have used, as if in a state of identification with me rather than developing their own capacities to think about the patients.

After about a year it was clear how much less preoccupied the GPs were with referring patients whom I would consider suitable for psychotherapy and that they were more comfortable with bringing patients they wanted help in thinking about. It emerged that the GPs individually collected particular types of patients and referred them to me for particular reasons. For example, one of the partners felt insecure in his psychiatric experience while he was a GP trainee and described how very disturbed patients seemed to "wrap themselves around him" and make increasing demands, which he felt ill-equipped to manage; as a result he over-compensated by offering them more and more time.

The development of the relationship between the GPs and me was reflected over time in a different quality to the referral letters. There was less detail of the patient's medical history and mental state in a psychiatric sense and more description of the effect the patient had on the doctor, such as making them feel anxious, hopeless, frustrated, or confused. In return, I could feel clearer about what was behind the referral and how my response could try to address and understand this. In discussions with me, the GPs emphasized how they valued having psychodynamic formulations in their patients' notes to refer to.

Case study: "Tom"

An example of how it became increasingly possible to think about patients and why they may have been referred was a young psychotic man I shall call Tom. Tom was very articulate and middle class, with a psychiatric history characterized by denial of the severity of his illness and attempts to treat him with counselling and antidepressants. He was referred to me, and I recommended that he be referred to the catchment area's psychiatric team. At the time there was a sense that the GP was embarrassed at having referred this patient to the psychotherapist and not a psychiatrist in the first instance. At the review meeting, however, it was possible to come back to this and to be more in contact with the tragedy of the situation, in which both professionals and the patient's family came to be caught up in the denial of the nature of his illness. In discussing this, there was an experience in the room of a brief contact with something of the painfulness and pressures of their patients' experiences to which GPs are exposed—and also a moment that seemed to capture a more realistic depressive position in relation to my presence as a therapist.

The caseload

Early in the placement in the practice there was a rapid rate of referrals, which included some particularly anxiety-provoking cases. I felt that the GPs were letting me know something of the pressures and demands to which they were exposed in their daily work. The level of need and disturbance of the patients felt persecutory, and I experienced a struggle not to book my time in the surgery so fully that it was not possible to think about the patients. With time, the referral rate slowed down, and there was more opportunity to discuss patients prior to referral. Over time I became aware that the GPs tended not to refer patients who went to them requesting referrals for private psychotherapy in what seemed quite a straightforward way; they simply put these patients in contact with a suitable organization. In addition, other patients were referred by the GPs to the psychology department of the local hospital for behavioural and cognitive therapies. This seemed to give further support to the emerging view that the GPs were referring patients to me because of something particularly troubling to them in their relationship with the patient, which they wanted help in thinking about.

Referrals were varied and included patients with depression, anxiety, and relationship and personality difficulties similar to patients seen in an outpatient psychotherapy department. There were also patients referred or discussed the nature of whose difficulties was somewhat less akin to a recognizable "psychotherapy referral" but seemed to reside in their particular ability to arouse anxiety, often of a particularly persecutory nature, in their doctors. These included paranoid, suicidal, and addicted patients and those whose problems were especially worrying as they affected young children in their care. The degree of disturbance and deprivation of these patients was considerable, and I was particularly struck early on in my work in the practice by the referral of several patients with very severe depression and high risk of suicide. These were patients with very little capacity to feel some hope and pursue a relationship with a psychotherapist. They all ceased to attend after one or two appointments, and I felt the referrals in part represented a wish for me to know something of the burden of despair and hopelessness as well as the perverse relationships to which GPs' patients can expose them.

There was considerable variation in the outcomes of the referrals. Early on, a number of patients never returned, or, having got to the point of referral to a psychotherapist elsewhere, they never took this up. It is possible that this in part reflected the greater degree of disturbance of some of the patients first referred, but this may also have reflected my own position. At the time I was still seeing my role in the surgery rather as doing a psychotherapy-department-style assessment. On reflection this did not seem to be the most helpful model in the primary care setting, where the task

more pertinently seemed to be one of both experiencing and thinking about the patient and finding a way then of talking to both the
patient and the GP about the difficulties that were being presented.
The reality for many of the patients seen was that any experience of
psychotherapy they had was to be in the GP surgery. As a therapist, I could see patients mainly for brief interventions or more
open-ended intermittent contact, and only a few of them for
monthly or fortnightly work for periods of a year to eighteen
months. I therefore learned to be quite flexible in what was offered
to patients and was more likely to take them on for short-term
work than patients seen in the psychotherapy department. Of the
patients referred, only two were placed on a waiting list for group
or individual treatment in the psychotherapy department. A small
number of patients did move on to more intensive psychoanalytic
treatments elsewhere.

GP notes

Issues of confidentiality and patients' consent to information being
gathered and recorded about them are complex and unclear when
seeing patients for a psychodynamic interview in a setting that is
primarily not about psychotherapy but where intimate information
about the patient is available. In this setting I was provided with
the GP notes of the patients referred, and I used them. These could
contain a mine of information, often dating back to the patient's
birth and early infancy. In addition to information about psychosomatic aspects of the patient's presentation and the use they made of
GPs, at times essential and almost lost pieces of information
emerged.

Case study: "Barbara"

An example of such a case was Barbara, a young woman who
came to see me only after considerable difficulty, telephoning
the psychotherapy department and consulting her GP, wanting
to know exactly my relationship with the practice, her perma-
nence there, and the meaning of an "assessment". Underlying

the referral was the GP's concern at her rage at the GP's perceived unavailability to her.

After a very difficult and somewhat puzzling consultation I was able to look in her notes and saw a small piece of paper tucked at the back, documenting her fostering—not her adoption—at the age of 18 months, after her mother had left her. The patient's deep sense of shame in relation to this had led to its denial in her mind as an event of significance, although her devastation and fury at perceived slights and rejections were clearly enacted in the primary care setting. It is possible that this information might have emerged over time, but its availability in the notes led rapidly to a different understanding of her difficulties as she presented those to her GP and to me.

Arguably, looking in the patients' notes breached a boundary, as the patient had not given explicit consent to this; but when I raised the fact that I had discovered information in this way, patients seemed to have had an expectation that their notes would have been available to me and indeed seemed to feel contained by it. The notes could make fascinating reading, and the contents, although available, were often not known by the GP. At times this put me in the position of knowing something about the patient that they had not told me, other than perhaps by giving an unconscious cue that prompted my curiosity and sent me back to the notes. This illustrates one of the ways in which working in primary care is quite "dirty work", involving a stepping out from psychoanalytic technique, strictly speaking, when other sources of information about the patients' histories, relationships, and functioning are available in the setting. I also recorded my contact with patients in the GP notes, and there were opportunities for the doctors to make links between these appointments and what the patients may subsequently present to them.

The practice as patient

There is a body of literature about counselling in primary care and a smaller body about psychoanalytic psychotherapy in this setting, with emphasis on the need to be flexible (Brook & Temperley, 1976;

Temperley, 1978 ; Wiener & Sher, 1998). However, it seems that this is a particular kind of flexibility within which one has to be very clear about one's own boundaries and to have a firm internal model of the work. General practice involves working in an atmosphere of intense neediness and demand, and primitive anxieties and defences can ricochet around. It can be extremely difficult for a psychotherapeutic stance to be maintained outside the four walls of a psychotherapy department and within an environment where one's presence can arouse feelings of considerable envy and threat. In primary care there is a wealth of clinical experience and an opportunity to develop one's role as a psychotherapist, involving really having to think, sometimes on one's toes, about what is being requested or enacted and why. Making a shift from representing a fragment of a psychotherapy department in a GP's surgery to feeling in a different position—more of a hinterland in relation to them, in which the therapist is not part of the primary care team but is in an intimate relation to them—can place the therapist in an exposed position but also one that allows the necessary space to think.

The state of mind of the practice as regards their work as GPs and their ability to tolerate the uncertainties and anxieties of the psychoanalytic world while also recognizing its value as something helpful to them is crucial in determining what can be achieved by the presence of a psychotherapist in the practice. Members of the practice described in this chapter seemed to have a genuine wish to understand and to learn more of their patients' difficulties and how these presented in psychodynamic terms, involving some scrutiny of their own feelings and responses while, by and large, staying in role as the patients' GP. This allowed some change in the GPs' anxiety and feelings of persecution, which I also felt my presence could evoke. Another practice may request the presence of a psychotherapist more as a wish to split off and defend themselves against thinking about their patients, and this may impose significant limitations on how the therapist can function. Hence, what is being presented to the therapist by the practice as a whole, both in terms of patients referred and other conscious and unconscious communications, needs to be understood as part of the task of the therapist. This allows the possibility of engaging with the practice and being in close contact with the GPs without being overly identified with them. It is from this position that the therapist is then able to gain some understanding of the problem and the nature of the help the GPs want and to find a way to talk to them in an effective way about this. This is, of course, essential in working psychoanalytically with a patient.

It might seem as if thinking of the practice as a patient is to pathologize it or be pejorative. This is not the intention but, rather, to acknowledge—as in other areas of applied psychoanalytic work—that the organizational dynamics are as worthy of attention and consideration as the clinical material or what is more overtly presented. Supervision has an important role to play, both for individual patients and for the institutional dynamics. Enid Balint wrote about the role of the psychotherapist in primary care and emphasized that the purpose is not to provide the GPs with a psychotherapy training but, rather, to help them to be more fully themselves in their work (E. Balint et al., 1993; Elder, 1996). It seems that this task involves therapists being clear in their own role in order to support the GPs in theirs.

CHAPTER ELEVEN

Bridging the gap: experiences at the interface of primary care and a psychotherapy institution

Sue Blake

The problem with belonging to two institutions is that neither side fully understands the perspective of the other; working across boundaries is difficult and can be dispiriting at times, but there are great rewards when human connections are achieved.

In the summer of 2001 I was appointed to work as a senior lecturer in primary care in the Adult Department of the Tavistock Clinic. This is a challenging position, at the interface of two important and well-established specialities within the health service—mental health and primary care—made all the more demanding by the recent changes in organization and a requirement on both sides to coordinate services. I am based in the Clinic for half of the week; for the rest of my time I am a partner in a large, busy inner-city practice in north Islington, where I have worked for over twelve years. Before working as a GP, I was a psychiatrist for many years, and during that time I also trained as a psychoanalytical psychotherapist. So I have a foot in several camps, which could be experienced as having split loyalties and creating confusion in my professional identity. To work effectively across the boundary, it has been important to me personally—having combined potentially conflicting approaches in my training—to understand both perspectives from the inside. It is from this background that some of the following thoughts and ideas have emerged.

The relationship between primary care and mental health services has assumed particular significance since the publication of the *National Service Framework for Mental Health* (Department of Health (1999). There are, for example, standards laid down requiring that any service user with a common mental health problem who contacts their Primary Health Care Team (PHCT) should have their needs identified and assessed and be offered effective treatments if they require these, including referral to specialist services for further assessment, treatment, and care. Given current resources, it could be thought that these requirements are unrealistic. They certainly impose a far greater demand on services in both primary care and specialist departments and necessitate close working between the two.

The Tavistock Clinic is the main centre for psychotherapy training in the National Health Service and as such provides a "centre of excellence" service that is more specialized than that of a psychotherapy department in a district general hospital. It has always worked hard to sustain its relationship with primary care, and it receives the majority of its referrals from GPs. My role as GP in the adult department, where psychoanalytic psychotherapy is the treatment modality, is to help both sides manage the boundary between primary care and psychotherapy.

Psychoanalytic psychotherapy makes systematic use of the relationship between therapist and patient to produce a change in the patient's cognition, feelings, and behaviour. It uses the arousal and analysis of emotions directed towards the therapist as the central vehicle of change, and this has particular implications for the management of this boundary. Long-term individual work offers the opportunity to grapple with longstanding problems and thereby to break cycles of behaviour, and working in depth with a few people can effect change that benefits more than just the patient in treatment. But, of course, the psychotherapist, working in this way for at least part of the time, sees a few patients exclusively and in a sense has to block out all those other people in need who cannot be fitted in. The paradox here is that having long-term patients can actually facilitate a therapist's ability to do short-term work and thus see a greater number of patients. So we are left with the problem of how to ration this scarce resource and how to find the patients who can use it best.

Patients with a wide variety of mental health problems may be suitable for psychotherapy, but the incidence of psychological morbidity far outstrips the availability of psychotherapy services throughout the country. Common disorders such as depression, anxiety, eating and personality disorders, and psychosomatic illness are considered amenable to psychotherapy, whereas in some more severe conditions, such as schizophrenia and other psychotic illnesses, psychological approaches would be seen as an adjunct to pharmacological therapies. However, with the shift away from hospitals to care in the community, more mentally ill patients are becoming the responsibility of primary care services. To lessen their burden, GPs are referring more severe cases for psychotherapy in the hope that something can be done. Gone are the days of the "worried well". Freud's old maxim that psychoanalysis could be used to "turn neurotic misery into normal human unhappiness" is a luxury of the past, as psychotherapy departments respond to the changing needs of GPs and other referrers. My descriptions of the changing interface between the Tavistock and primary care may be recognized by many readers working in NHS psychotherapy departments, especially those with a training role.

Establishing links

When I joined the department, my first task was to establish my own links—clinically, administratively, and educationally—with my new colleagues. The Adult Department is divided for purposes of clinical work into three units, each providing a sectorized service to their referrers in primary care. I became attached to one of these. I started to attend the weekly clinical meeting and, more importantly for my purposes, established a base from which to develop new approaches in forming clinical links.

Historically the department has had specific links with some practices through the placement of a therapist in those practices for a period of time. This can lead to a developing relationship with the practices, but pivotal is the relationship with the GPs concerned, and it is essential that there are regular meetings between the latter and the therapist. This is an effective and rewarding way of working, but it involves a considerable amount of work and commitment. It also leads to an increased number of referrals. On our unit we therefore began to look at ways of rationalizing the entire range of referrals that came in in order to clarify how to use our unique position as an applied psychoanalytic service. Another factor here was the arrival of the primary care trusts (PCTs), which had responsibility for commissioning all mental health services. Newly formed PCTs were engaged in consultation exercises, and so it seemed a good time to firm up links with key GP practices, and with primary care generally.

When I first began to work there, the Adult Department was referred just over 800 patients a year, almost all from primary care. These patients came mainly from within local PCTs, but some also came from further afield. Each unit applied its own criteria for distribution, but in essence referrals arrived in the hands of a nominated unit member each week for distribution. This referrals coordinator did some work, including telephoning GPs, practice counsellors, or psychiatrists, before the referrals were allocated within the units, in a fairly arbitrary manner. This preliminary work often involved leaving unanswered messages at unknown practices—a time-consuming and inefficient pastime.

Within our own unit we proposed a shift: to develop sectorization further, so that each individual therapist within the unit would take referrals regularly from specific practices. From the GP's point of view, having a named link person to contact might establish a helpful human connection and lead to those patients who could most appropriately use our service being referred. This arrangement has been helpful, but it does not overcome every problem. I am reminded of a very telling situation in which I found myself, when a primary care colleague had referred a patient, and the referral had, for various reasons, been considered inappropriate. However, the method of referring the patient back to his GP had been equally inappropriate: a letter sent to the patient had referred him back to his GP without any explanation, and the GP had also received no explanation of what, in his terms, he experienced as a "rejection" of his long-considered referral. Indeed, it is usually the case that most primary care referrals are the product of much thought and deliberation on the part of the referrer. So it was in this case.

In this situation, I became the arbitrator, explaining, on the one hand, to my GP colleague that a great deal of thought would have gone into this decision not to take on the patient—even for an assessment—and at the same time trying to help my other colleague at the Tavistock understand how a GP might find it difficult, if possible at all, to explain to their patient why they were not to be seen at the Tavistock—which for many who know of the institution is also seen as a rejection verging on an insult.

One problem for GP colleagues is that they expect something useful from a referral, even if the case is not to be taken on. They are looking for an opinion, some guidance on management, in order to continue their work with the patient in primary care. When this is not forthcoming, it can feel difficult, knowing that a GP is going to feel let down and trying to explain to him or her the pressures that mean that the department has to protect itself and its style of working, and that sometimes the answer has to be no. I remember a particular GP colleague who spelled it out to me quite simply: "I'm at the end of the line, I've tried everything with this patient, I just want some help from somebody." In that situation I was in a position to facilitate a conversation between GP and consultant that helped the GP to simply carry on seeing the patient in the surgery, which is sometimes all that can be done. But there is a lingering sense, I know, among primary care colleagues that there is some knowledge held at the Tavistock that is experienced as not being shared—leading to resentment in those left to continue the ongoing care of the patients.

In addition to holding this role as a member of a clinical unit, I quickly became involved with the primary care seminar—a clinic-wide meeting that provides space for therapists from all departments to consider their primary-care-based work from different perspectives. The challenge was to try to generate new interest and improve membership. This has worked well. It seems that these seminars offer the opportunity to share the difficulties that staff and senior trainees run into in settings away from the security of the Tavistock. They also offer support and understanding, particularly in relation to the sense of isolation so often encountered when working away from the home institution. The group has met with increasing frequency, and presentations have covered most of the attachments described in this book, as well as primary care research being carried out in the clinic.

These structures helped me to understand from the inside how the process works for the setting up of psychotherapy for a patient referred from primary care, and I began to experience the problems as they present at the interface between the two worlds of primary care and psychotherapy. The rules and boundaries about patients who can and cannot be seen became clearer as I took part in the clinical meetings, while still remaining aware as a GP of the tension that exists when I am unable to cope any longer with a patient— and sometimes still yearning simply for a referral to be accepted— whether or not it is "appropriate"! I can feel very torn between my roles: on the one hand working to expand networks—creating more referrals—and on the other rationing them so as not to create an unmanageable workload. The psychotherapists dealing with referrals to the department may be similarly split, but they are not so acutely involved in what happens when these are not accepted. It must also be admitted that there is a natural wish in psychotherapy institutions to reject the very patients whom GPs most want to hand over. Referral criteria are a legitimate way of processing the dread of being taken over by the impact of seriously disturbed people who—in truth—cannot be satisfactorily helped. As a GP within this psychotherapy department, I can remind my colleagues what GPs have to deal with in the community and what support they need from the specialist in the institution. Most importantly, though, the daily movement across the two worlds and experiencing the contrasts in ways of working brings me in touch with the human difficulties in this sort of work and with the insolubility of some aspects of it.

Further developments

In my first nine months of working in the post, I had been guided by a helpful member of staff in the Adult Department, but she did not have designated sessions for primary care work. Subsequently a consultant psychotherapist was appointed with a job description that included a specific remit to develop links with primary care. Following her arrival, a new and particularly productive period of activity began. This perhaps reflects the importance of regular working together by a member of staff from each of the two worlds. Probably the most important initiative was the formalizing of our meetings and the establishment of a departmental primary care group. This is now an active and cohesive group within the department. It functions to reflect upon the links and work within primary care and to develop our networks.

The central membership of this primary care group is myself and the consultant, but this was quickly extended to include the department manager and two to three other staff members who have specific primary care roles. Frequently there are invited guests or department members, including interested trainees. The group meets fortnightly, on a Monday morning, and has become an established part of the timetable as a space, in part at least, to reflect on the clinical and training work in progress.

We soon began to realize that much work was already being done throughout the institution by individuals or small groups who were often unaware of each other. The effect of this was that contact with primary care could be patchy or even be duplicated. Several examples of discovering such duplication resulted in the unravelling of arrangements for similar types of workshops or conferences that were being set up, with different staff members inevitably knocking on the same doors of already overloaded professionals. Some of this confusion arose from the fact that there are three departments within the Clinic, each functioning to some extent autonomously. The success of the group in addressing this problem has really come from recognizing the need to coordinate and map out our primary care activity and to include all departments across the clinic in many of our meetings.

The next area we reviewed was one that I had already looked at: the fundamental business of the communication and links that we have with our referrers in primary care. The link clinician scheme described above had been an early attempt at rationalizing our system, but it had been only partially successful. There remained several difficulties. Up until the time when a patient arrived at the unit, there was often no place or space for either the departmental manager (a non-clinician) or the referrals coordinator (a junior member of staff) to bring the referral for thought or discussion. Straightforward telephone calls to GPs in order to request further information were therefore in many cases rapidly becoming complicated by political, contractual, or clinical issues of which the manager or co-coordinator concerned might not previously have been aware. We therefore proposed a separate referrals meeting to address some of these issues.

We have now set up a referrals meeting that provides the space to think about the vital initial contact with the referrer. The membership includes myself, the primary care consultant, the departmental manager, and the referrals coordinator. Each referral can now be discussed prior to any contact being made. In this way the knowledge, experience, and links with referrers can be retained within the whole group rather than just lodged in one person, who might then leave the unit. The meeting takes place in the half-hour before the unit meeting, but it does not take over the role of the unit meeting. Instead, it attends to an aspect of the referrals process that until then had remained hidden.

The last development piloted on this unit has been to use a proforma to let our referrers know what information we require. As a result, we now only have to interrupt referrers and ask more questions for a good clinical reason. The use of a proforma provides GPs with a ready reminder both of the service offered and also of what might be relevant information about the patient to the assessing psychotherapist. More subtly, we hope to let our referrers know that we are trying to improve our service to them and our communication with them. This also creates a process whereby an unconscious view of referrers as needy importuners who break into the smooth running of the department can change into a more adult view of them as colleagues in the care of patients, as well as providing our bread and butter.

Training

There remains the question of training initiatives: an area in which the Tavistock traditionally plays a leading role, devoting many of its resources to the organization of conferences, workshops, and training programmes. Politically there has been an increasing focus on the needs of primary care professionals for adequate support, supervision, and training in the area of mental health. Clinical governance and the need for continued professional development and appraisal have become an integral part of general practice. However, alongside these political changes, there has unfortunately been an increasing trend to place inexperienced workers in the front line of primary care. This rather short-term political expediency further highlights the need for integrated and developed training experiences for a variety of health care professionals. Currently no substantial training based on psychoanalytic thinking exists for such workers, nor indeed is there anything available to nourish those already committed to this way of working.

My first venture in this area has therefore been to reinstate the regular half-day conferences for primary care professionals on common clinical problems and dilemmas. We started with a conference entitled "Depression in Primary Care: Stuck Patient or Stuck Doctor?" We invited both a psychoanalyst from the Adult Department and an academic GP to speak on the subject of "heart-sink patients"—a topic that was chosen to highlight the seeming insolubility to the GP of some patients' problems. In the format of such conferences there is a fine balance between informative talks and the opportunity to join in discussing clinical material in group sessions. GPs need the space to do some grumbling, to share the sense of frustration and hopelessness that dealing with some patients can bring, before their minds are free to take in new ideas.

The ongoing work in the Balint tradition continues, with some changes in form and membership but essentially cherishing the same ideals. At the time of writing, there remains one Balint group running at the Tavistock—one of the very few remaining of its type in the country altogether. But we have also developed a modified version of the work discussion group: a forum for GPs, counsellors, and other primary care workers to present their work in detail and discuss the setting and its effect on their practice. This group caters for the need for all professionals involved in treating psychological problems to have regular supervision of their work. We are also setting up two-termly meetings where GP registrars in their final year of postgraduate training will also be able to bring their current clinical problems for help and supervision. As they begin to think about their future in general practice, we believe it is important for them to build up resources to manage the deluge of patients they will encounter through their careers, few of whom can be offered psychotherapy.

We are also now developing a new form of introductory training course for primary care workers on common mental health issues from a psychodynamic perspective. This will be open to GPs, practice nurses, counsellors, and the new primary care mental health workers. This is a joint venture with the primary care section of the Association of Psychoanalytic Psychotherapy, as part of a scheme that may allow the development over time of a range of training activities for primary care professionals. The approach is based on a realistic recognition of the present situation for training in primary care. We will start initially to focus on the development of an advanced training for supervisors and experienced professionals in primary care.

From the other direction, there is now some primary care input to the Tavistock psychoanalytic trainings and in particular a regular seminar on letter-writing to GPs, offered on a termly basis to trainees. These give me an opportunity to feed back from a GP's perspective how the letters written back from a therapist might sound to a GP and how they might help in managing the patient. There is now a whole-term course on primary care when psychotherapy trainees are encouraged to visit a primary care setting and to report back on their experiences, to help them make sense of the world their patients and referrers inhabit. I see my role here as helping trainees to shift from thinking exclusively about the internal world of their patients to looking at their external world and how that can be negotiated.

As a GP, it has certainly been interesting to find myself occasionally face to face with the therapist who had been seeing one of my patients and holding a copy of a letter—already perhaps read by myself or one of my GP colleagues—and actually to have a conversation about someone we both know so well in such different ways. Of course, this was only a chance occurrence in a whole system of training, but it was nevertheless fascinating and influenced how I viewed such a patient the next time they presented in my surgery.

Conclusions

What, if any, part of this work is effective, and to what extent does it answer the questions we are being asked? At a meeting with the Trust board of directors, I was asked which of the activities I had described was most useful—and if I could do only one thing, which would it be? I had no difficulty in replying that my single most useful activity is the referrals meeting. It seems to me that a fuller involvement in how a psychotherapy service deals with its cases makes me better equipped to facilitate the relationship between primary and secondary services.

However, no amount of understanding can reduce the compelling burden of care that is made on the primary care workers. The risk that is obvious to those working at this interface of primary and secondary services is that each is in danger of not recognizing the values of the other service in relation to the patient. It is a great irony that in a world where understanding and intuition are valued so highly, we often seem least to understand our own interactions. In the effort to do the best for our patients, we can end up at odds with each other, unless we are careful to apply to ourselves the psychoanalytic thinking we use so freely on these patients.

So how are we to go forward, in this NHS that is ever more demanding of our time, our wits, and our IT skills? In primary care, the burden can only be expected to increase, and the fear is that more and more workers will suffer burnout as they struggle to cope. Many GPs and other primary care professionals are in their jobs precisely because they enjoy the emotional interaction with patients and its intensity. They need more support, supervision, and nurturing if they are to continue to produce what the NHS demands of them. Only with the sort of approach that started with Balint and has since undergone so many adaptations and taken on so many different forms can they be expected to go on. There is indeed an "inverse care" law (Tudor Hart, 1988): that GPs, practice nurses, and health visitors often have to manage by themselves with the most complex and intractable cases because an onward referral is not practical or acceptable to either patient or psychotherapy specialist. It may be that our internal difficulties as professionals match the inter-institutional difficulties, but we have to learn to provide "care for the carers" as a matter of routine, not just in emergencies when professionals are at the point of burnout. With a psychotherapeutic understanding we can surely work together in supporting each other and reducing the overall burden.

REFERENCES

Agger, I. (1994). *The Blue Room*. London: Zed Books.

Altschuler, J. (1997). *Working with Chronic Illness*. London: Macmillan.

Andersen, T. (2004). Consultations to professionals and families where there is psychosis. *Context, 72* (April): 26–28.

Andersen, T. (1987). The reflecting team: Dialogue and meta-dialogue in clinical work. *Family Process, 26*: 415–428.

Andersen, T. (Ed.) (1990). *The Reflecting Team*. Broadstairs: Borgmann.

Appelfeld, E. (2001). The dread: An essay on communication across cultural boundaries. *International Journal of Critical Psychology, 4*: 19–34

Balbernie, R. (2002). An infant mental health service: The importance of the early years and evidence-based practice. Available on the website of the Association for Infant Mental Health (www.aimh .org.uk).

Balint, E., & Norrell, J. (Eds.) (1973). *Six Minutes for the Patient*. London: Tavistock.

Balint, E., Courtenay, M., Elder, A., Hull, S., & Julian, P. (1993). *The Doctor, the Patient and the Group: Balint Revisited*. London: Routledge.

Balint, M. (1957). *The Doctor, His Patient and the Illness*. London: Pitman.

Barrows, P. (1999). Brief work with under fives: A psychoanalytic approach. *Clinical Child Psychology and Psychiatry, 4*: 240–260.

Barrows, P. (2000). Making the case for dedicated infant mental health services. *Psychoanalytic Psychotherapy, 14*: 111–128.

Bion, W. R. (1962). *Learning from Experience.* London: Heinemann.

Blount, A., & Bayona, J. (1994). Towards a system of integrated primary care. *Family Systems Medicine, 12*: 171–182

Bor, R., & McCann, D. (Eds.) (1999). *The Practice of Counselling in Primary Care.* London: Sage.

Boss, P. (1991). Ambiguous loss. In: F. Walsh & M. McGoldrick (Eds.), *Living Beyond Loss.* London: Norton.

Bourdieu, P. (1990). *The Logic of Practice.* Cambridge: Polity.

Brah, A. (1996). *Cartographies of Diaspora.* London: Routledge.

Brook, A. (1978). An aspect of community mental health: Consultative work with general practice teams. *Health Trends, 10* (2): 37–40

Brook, A., & Temperley, J. (1976). The contribution of a psychotherapist to general practice. *Journal of the Royal College of General Practitioners, 26*: 86–94.

Burton, J., & Launer, J. (2003). *Supervision and Support in Primary Care*: Oxford: Radcliffe.

Cecchin, G. (1987). Hypothesising, circularity and neutrality revisited: An invitation to curiosity. *Family Process, 26*: 405–413.

Corney, R. (1993). Studies of the effectiveness of counselling in general practice. In: R. Corney & R. Jenkins (Eds.), *Counselling in General Practice.* London: Routledge.

Corney, R. (1996). The role of counselling in primary prevention. In: T. Kendrick, A. Tylee, & P. Freeling (Eds.), *The Prevention of Mental Illness in Primary Care.* Cambridge: Cambridge University Press.

Cox, J. L., Holden, J. M., & Sagovsky, R. (1987). Detection of postnatal depression. *British Journal of Psychiatry, 150*: 782–786.

Daws, D. (1985). Standing next to the weighing scales. *Journal of Child Psychotherapy, 11*: 77–85.

Daws, D. (1993). *Through the Night: Helping Parents and Sleepless Infants.* London: Free Association Books.

Daws, D. (1995). Psychotherapy in the community. In: J. Trowell & M. Bower (Eds.), *The Emotional Needs of Young Children and Their Families.* London: Routledge.

De Shazer, S. (1985). *Keys to Solution in Brief Therapy.* New York: Norton.

Department for Education and Skills (2003). *Every Child Matters.* Available at www.dfes.gov.uk/everychildmatters

Department of Health (1995). *Together We Stand: The Commissioning, Role and Management of Child and Adolescent Mental Health Services.* London: Her Majesty's Stationery Office.

Department of Health (1999). *National Service Framework for Mental Health: Modern Standards and Service Models.* London.

Department of Health (2002). *Improvement, Expansion and Reform: The Next Three Years, Priorities and Planning Framework 2003–2006.* London.

Department of Health (2004). *National Service Framework for Children, Young People and Maternity Services.* London.

Douglas, J., & Richman, N. (1984). *My Child Won't Sleep.* Harmondsworth: Penguin.

Dwivedi, K. (Ed.) (1999). Sowing the seeds of cultural competence. *Context, 44* (special edition).

East, P. (1995). *Counselling in Medical Settings.* Milton Keynes: Open University Press.

Elder, A. (1986). Psychotherapy in general practice. In: H. Maxwell (Ed.), *Psychotherapy: An Outline for Trainee Psychiatrists, Medical Students and Practitioners.* London: Whurr.

Elder, A. (1987). Moments of change. In: A. Elder & O. Samuel (Eds.), *While I'm Here, Doctor: A Study of the Doctor Patient Relationship.* London: Tavistock Press.

Elder, A. (1996). Enid Balint's contribution to general practice. *Psychoanalytic Psychotherapy, 10*: 101–108.

Falicov, C. (1998). *Latino Families in Therapy.* New York: Guilford Press.

Fog Olwig, K. (1999). Narratives of the children left behind: Home and identity in globalised Caribbean families. *Journal of Ethnic and Migration Studies, 25*: 267–284.

Fonagy, P. (1998). Prevention, the appropriate target of infant psychotherapy. *Infant Mental Health Journal, 19*: 124–150.

Garralda, M. E., & Bailey, D. (1986). Children with psychiatric disorders in primary care. *Journal of Child Psychology and Psychiatry, 27*: 611–624.

Garralda, M. E., Bowman, F. M., & Mandalia, S. (1999). Children with psychiatric disorders who are frequent attenders to primary care. *European Child and Adolescent Psychiatry, 8*: 34–44.

Gladstone, A., & Slack, J. (2003). Childcare practice and early years education: Does thinking about infant mental health make a difference? *AIMH (UK) Newsletter, 3*: 4–5.

Goldberg, D., & Huxley, P. (1992). *Common Mental Disorders.* London: Routledge.

Gosling, R., & Turquet, P. (1964). The training of general practitioners. In: R. Gosling, D. Miller, D. Woodhouse, & P. Turquet (Eds.), *The Use of Small Groups in Training*. London: Codicote.

Graham, H., & Sher, M. (1976). Social work in general practice. *Journal of the Royal College of General Practitioners, 26*: 95–105.

Graham, H., Senior, R., Lazarus, M., Mayer, R., & Asen, K. (1992). Family therapy in general practice: Views of referrers and clients. *British Journal of General Practice, 42*: 25–28.

Greenhalgh, T., & Hurwitz, B. (1998). *Narrative-Based Medicine: Dialogue and Discourse in Clinical Practice*. London: BMJ Books.

Grier, F. (Ed.) (2004). *Oedipus and the Couple*. London: Karnac.

Habermas, J. (1990). *Moral Consciousness and Communicative Action*. Cambridge: Polity Press.

Hale, R., & Hudson, L. (1992). The Tavistock study of young doctors: Report of the pilot phase. *British Journal of Hospital Medicine, 47*: 452–464.

Ham, D. C. (1993). Empathy. In: J. H. Chin, J. H. Liem, M. D. C. Ham, & G. K. Hong (Eds.), *Transference and Empathy in Asian American Psychotherapy: Cultural Values and Treatment Needs*. Westport, CT: Greenwood Press.

Harré, R. (1986). An outline of the social constructionist viewpoint. In: R. Harré (Ed.), *The Social Construction of Emotions*. Oxford: Blackwell.

Hartman, E. (1973). *The Functions of Sleep*. New Haven, CT: Yale University Press.

Hoag, L. (1992). Psychotherapy in the GP surgery: Considerations of the frame. *British Journal of Psychotherapy, 8*: 417–423.

Holden, J. H., Sagovsky, R., & Cox, J. L. (1989). Counselling in general practice settings: Controlled study of health visitor intervention in treatment of postnatal depression. *British Medical Journal, 298*: 223–226.

Hopkins, R. (2002). *Narrative, Culture and Power: A Systemic Perspective on Cross-Cultural Communication in General Practice*. Masters Thesis, Tavistock Clinic.

Huffington, C., Armstrong, D., Halton, W., Hoyle, L., & Pooley, J. (2004). *Working Below the Surface: The Emotional Life of Contemporary Organisations*. London: Karnac.

Keithley, J., Bond, T., & Marsh, G. (2002). *Counselling in Primary Care* (2nd edition). Oxford: Oxford University Press.

Kelleher, D., & Hillier, S. (1996). *Researching Cultural Differences in Health*. London: Routledge.

Kleinman, A. (1988). *The Illness Narratives: Suffering, Healing and the Human Condition*. New York: Basic Books.

Krause, I. (1998). *Therapy across Culture*. London: Sage.

Launer, J. (1994a). Psychotherapy in the general practitioner surgery: Working with and without a secure therapeutic frame. *British Journal of Psychotherapy, 11*: 120–126.

Launer, J. (1994b). What do general practitioners want? *Tavistock Gazette, 39*: 14–19.

Launer, J. (1996). Towards systemic general practice. *Context, 26*: 42–45.

Launer, J. (2002). *Narrative-Based Primary Care: A Practical Guide*. Oxford: Radcliffe.

Launer, J., & Lindsey, C. (1997). Training for systemic general practice: A new approach from the Tavistock Clinic. *British Journal of General Practice, 47*: 453–456.

Lees, J. (Ed.) (1999). *Clinical Counselling in Primary Care*. London: Routledge.

Lester, H., Glasby, J., & Tylee, A. (2004). Integrated primary mental health care: Threat or opportunity in the new NHS? *British Journal of General Practice, 54*: 285–291.

Lock, J. (2002). Treating adolescents with eating disorders in the family context: Empirical and theoretical considerations. *Child and Adolescent Psychiatric Clinics of North America, 11*: 331–342.

Loshak, R. (2003). Working with Bangladeshi young women. *Psychoanalytic Psychotherapy, 17*: 52–67.

Louden, P., & Graham, H. (1998). Working with an elderly couple. *Context, 12*: 39–43.

Malterud, K., & Kristiansen, U. (1995). The reflective metapositions of evaluation: A strategy for development of collaborative competence and clinical knowledge. *Family Systems Medicine, 13*: 79–89.

Mayer, R., & Graham, H. (1998). Getting your registrar to think families. *Education for General Practice, 9*: 234–237.

McDaniel, S. (2004). *Abstracts of Fifth European Congress of Family Therapy, Berlin*. Berlin: European Association for Family Therapy.

McDaniel, S., Hepworth, J., & Doherty, W. (1992). *Medical Family Therapy*. New York: Basic Books.

McDougall, J. (1986). *Theatres of the Mind*. London: Free Association Books.

McLeod, J. (1988). The work of counsellors in general practice. *Occasional Paper 37*. London: Royal College of General Practitioners.

Mellor-Clark, J., Simms-Ellis, R., & Burton, M. (2001). National Survey of Counsellors Working in Primary Care: Evidence for growing professionalism? *Occasional Paper 79*. London: Royal College of General Practitioners.

Merl, H. (1995). Reflecting supervision. *Journal of Systemic Therapies*, *14*: 47–56.

Miller, L. (2000). An Under-Fives Counselling Service and its relation to questions of assessment. In: M. Rustin & E. Quagliata (Eds.), *Assessment in Child Psychotherapy*. London: Duckworth.

Miller, L., Rustin, M., Rustin, M., & Shuttleworth, J. (Eds.) (1989). *Closely Observed Infants*. London: Duckworth.

Murray, L., & Cooper, P. J. (Eds.) (1997). *Postnatal Depression and Child Development*. London: Guilford Press.

Nemiah, J. C., & Sifneos, P. (1970). Affect and fantasy in patients with psychosomatic disorders. In: O. W. Hill (Ed.), *Modern Trends in Psychosomatic Medicine, Vol. 2*. London: Butterworth.

Obholzer, A., & Roberts, V. (Eds.) (1994). *The Unconscious at Work: Individual and Organizational Stress in the Human Services*. London: Routledge.

Palombo, S. (1978). *Dreaming and Memory*. New York: Basic Books.

Papadopoulos, R., & Byng-Hall, J. (Eds.) (1997). *Multiple Voices: Narrative in Systemic Family Psychotherapy*. London: Duckworth.

Papp, P. (1983). *The Process of Change*. New York: Guilford Press.

Pawliuk, N., Grizenko, N., Chan-Yip, A., Gantous, P., Mathew, J., & Nguyen, D. (1996). Acculturation style and psychological functioning in children of immigrants. *American Journal of Orthopsychiatry*, *66*: 111–121.

Phoenix, A. (2002). (Re)constructing gendered and ethnicised identities: Are we all marginal now? In: T. Johansson & O. Sernhede (Eds.), *Lifestyle, Desire and Politics: Contemporary Identities*. Gothenburg: Daidalos.

Pozzi, M. (2003). *Psychic Hooks and Bolts: Psychoanalytic Work with Children Under Five and Their Families*. London: Karnac.

Raval, H. (1996). A systemic perspective on working with interpreters. *Clinical Child Psychology and Psychiatry*, *1*: 29–43.

Rayner, E. (1999). Some functions of being fair and just—or not, in clinical psychoanalysis. *International Journal of Psychoanalysis*, *80*: 477–492.

Rhode, M., & Klauber, T. (Eds.) (2004). *The Many Faces of Asperger's Syndrome*. London: Karnac.

Roland, A. (1991). The self in cross-civilization perspective. In: R. Curtis (Ed.), *The Relational Self*. New York: Guildford Press.

Rolland, J. (1998). Beliefs and collaboration in illness: Evolution over time. *Families, Systems and Health, 16*: 7–26.

Salinsky, J., & Sackin, P. (2001). *How Are You Feeling, Doctor? Identifying and Avoiding Defensive Patterns in the Consultation.* Oxford: Radcliffe.

Seeley, S. (2001). Strengths and limitations of the Edinburgh Postnatal Depression Scale. In: *Postnatal Depression and Maternal Mental Health: A Public Health Priority.* Community Practitioners and Health Visitors Association Conference Proceedings, London, 2001.

Senior, R. (1994). Family therapy in general practice: "We have a clinic here on a Friday afternoon. . . ." *Journal of Family Therapy, 16*: 313–327.

Sher, M. (1977). Short-term contracts in general medical practice. In: J. Hutten (Ed.), *Short-term Contracts in Social Work.* London: Routledge & Kegan Paul.

Shonkoff, J. P., & Phillips, D. A. (Eds.) (2000). *From Neurons to Neighbourhoods: The Science of Early Child Development.* Washington, DC: National Academic Press.

Sibbald, B., Addington-Hall, J., Brenneman, D., & Freeling, P. (1993). Counsellors in English and Welsh general practices: Their nature and distribution. *British Medical Journal, 306*: 29–33.

Simpson, D., & Miller, L. (2004). *Unexpected Gains: Psychotherapy with People with Learning Difficulties.* London: Karnac.

Sluzki, C. (1979). Migration and family conflict. *Family Process, 18*: 379–390.

Stern, D. (1985). *The Interpersonal World of the Infant.* New York: Basic Books.

Storm, C., & Todd, T. (2001). Gaps between MFT supervision assumptions and common practice: Suggested best practice. *Journal of Marital and Family Therapy, 27*: 227–239.

Sutherland, J. (1957). An additional role for the psychological clinic. Appendix 4. In: M. Balint, *The Doctor, His Patient and the Illness.* London: Pitman.

Taylor, D. (Ed.) (1999). *Talking Cure: Mind and Method of the Tavistock Clinic.* London: Duckworth.

Temperley, J. (1978). Psychotherapy in the setting of general medical practice. *British Journal of Medical Psychology, 51*: 139–145.

Tudor Hart, J. (1988). *A New Kind of Doctor.* London: Merlin Press.

Waskett, C. (1999). Confidentiality in a team setting. In R. Bor & D. McCann (Eds.), *The Practice of Counselling in Primary Care.* London: Sage.

Wiener, J. (1996). Conference Proceedings: Future directions of psychotherapy in the NHS, adaptation or extinction. *Primary Care and Psychotherapy, 10* (Supplement).

Wiener, J., & Sher, M. (1998). *Counselling and Psychotherapy in Primary Health Care: A Psychodynamic Approach.* London: Macmillan.

White, M., & Epston, D. (1989). *Literate Means to Therapeutic Ends.* Dulwich: Dulwich Centre Publications.

White, M., & Epston, D. (1990). *Narrative Means to Therapeutic Ends.* New York: Norton.

Zalidis, S. (1994). The value of emotional awareness in general practice. In: A. Erskine & D. Judd (Eds.), *The Imaginative Body.* London: Whurr.

Zimmerman, J. L., & Beaudoin, M. (2002). Cats under the stars. *Child and Adolescent Mental Health 7*: 31–40.

INDEX